Iowa Kitchen Table Wisdom

ESSAYS OF HOPE AND
INSPIRATION FOR DIFFICULT
TIMES

Iowa Kitchen Table Wisdom

Essays of Hope and Inspiration for Difficult Times

By
J. L. Wertis

BEQUILLE PUBLISHING
Tulsa, Oklahoma, 74137

Cover Photo by Joel Drzycimski
Unsplash.com

Copyright © 2025 by J. L. Wertis
ISBN: 979-8-9990495-1-3
FIRST EDITION

COPYRIGHT AND DISTRIBUTION

The author retains the copyright including the manner in which the information is expressed.

This is a work of non-fiction. No names were changed, no characters created and no events fabricated. The events referenced are real, drawn from a variety of sources.

The author has endeavored to present the information in a journalistic manner. Psychological and philosophical subjects were researched against respected published works on the subject, but ultimately the conclusions reached were that of the author.

The author does not assume, and hereby disclaims, any liability, to any party, for errors or omissions, whatever the cause.

Dedicated to my mother who was always there to celebrate my successes in the good times, and to wipe away my tears during the difficult times. I will always treasure those moments we shared over a cup of tea at the kitchen table.

Contents

Preface 1
Introduction 5
You Can't Go Home Again 9
Nothing is Permanent Except Change 17
Don't Believe Everything You Hear 25
Commit Random Acts of Kindness 31
Judge Not, Lest Ye Be Judged 37
Some People Don't Want A Solution 43
You Can't Fix Stupid 51
Take the High Road 57
Embrace the Uncertainty 63
Life Begins at the End of Your Comfort Zone 69
Stop and Smell the Roses 73
No Good Deed Goes Unpunished 79
The Universe is Unfolding As It Should 85
Not My Circus, Not My Monkeys 91
When People Walk Away, Let Them 97
Be Yourself, Everyone Else is Taken 103
Protect Your Boundaries 109
Tough Times Don't Last, Tough People Do 115
Karma Can Be a Bitch 121

Let Your Life Speak 127
Picking at Old Wounds Won't Heal Them 133
Count Your Blessings 139
Live Simply, Love Richly 145
We're All in This Together 151
Let Peace Begin With Me 159
Forgiveness is For the Forgiver 167
Love Your Neighbor As Yourself 173
To Have a Friend Be One 179
Be Mindful in What You Do and Say 185
Live and Let Live 191
Stand Up For Your Principles 199
Never Lose Hope 207

Suggested Reading 217
About the Author 221

Preface

It's my observation that one of the greatest losses to American society is the kitchen table. Perhaps more things were resolved around America's kitchen tables than in any other place. For past generations, it was the heart of the home. Today's homes have kitchens with an island and no room for a table. We have even moved away from formal dining rooms and instead take our meals in front of the television set. Is it any wonder children no longer talk to their parents?

There was a time when every major event in life either took place or was discussed around the kitchen table. It was a place where political, financial, disciplinary, and personal issues were resolved.

It was a place where families, friends, and neighbors gathered to share a meal, play board games or cards, discuss events of the day, or just share their day over a cup of coffee or tea.

When life threw you a curve, a discussion with Mom over a cup of tea at the kitchen table seemed to make everything better.

I grew up in Iowa, and my grandparents on both sides were Iowa natives. Iowans are hardworking, practical people who are, as a whole, friendly, trusting, and honest and expect the same from others. I have fond memories of laughter, tears, inspiration, and celebrations around our humble kitchen table.

This book is a collection of short, thought-provoking essays that might have been the subject of discussion at the kitchen table in Iowa where I grew up. The essays are based on sayings and truisms as relevant now as they were back when kitchen tables were still a "thing."

The subject matter was inspired primarily by wise old proverbs, bible verses, maxims, and truisms passed down through the years. Some are based on advice given to me by good and loyal friends who helped me navigate troubled waters during my life. Some are newer, created by the younger generation or arising out of modern entertainment media such as movies or from

Preface

popular comedians. Some are just based on common sense. Wherever they originated, they hold the seeds of truth.

Although I didn't set out to share political content, it often was necessary. To dismiss or ignore the reality of the environment we currently live in, would be negligence on my part.

I hope you find inspiration and even an occasional chuckle as you peruse through these pages.

Welcome to my virtual kitchen table.

J.L. Wertis

IOWA KITCHEN TABLE WISDOM

INTRODUCTION

In these challenging times there's a lot to be anxious and stressed about. The future seems uncertain and unpredictable. Although we may be comforted by Martin Luther King Jr.'s claim that *"the arc of the moral universe is long, but it bends toward justice,"* we must admit that, right now, the end of that arc seems well out of sight!

Understanding how and why we got here matters. For those who know history, we are reminded that America was founded in violence. Political violence is as American as apple pie—and unfortunately, history shows that the violence sometimes is not just against external enemies, but against fellow citizens. However, a nation founded in violence is NOT destined to have a society that is violent. We can choose to be better. We MUST be better.

The following collection of timeless truths, ancient adages, and modern maxims are in no particular order. They can be read from first to last, randomly, or because the title intrigues or speaks to the reader's current interests.

The essays are my own, and any analysis or conclusion is based on my own experiences, education, and observations about the subject, which readers can choose to accept or ignore.

There is a "Suggested Reading List" section at the end of the book should you wish to further pursue a particular subject. Some are recently published, but there are also a few "classics" in the field of psychology and self-help. Many of the essays presented herein were inspired by ideas, concepts, and information in these books.

The goal is not to change any minds, politics, philosophies, views, or religious beliefs, but rather to create an environment for objectively observing and navigating the challenging time in which we are living. We all need to just stop, take a deep breath, shut out the voices in our head, and remember that we can, and will, get through this.

> *Don't believe what your eyes are telling you. All they show is limitation. Look with your understanding. Find out what*

INTRODUCTION

you already know and you will see the way to fly."
~Richard Bach
Jonathan Livingston Seagull

So, get comfortable, grab a cup of tea, imagine you are at your family's kitchen table, and let these inspirational essays renew you and give you hope and strength to face whatever the future holds.

Peace is not the end of the mundane, troublesome, and painful moments of life. Peace is found in the midst of the mundane, troublesome, and painful moments of life as we look for the good in all things, grasp tiny moments of joy glittering in the darkness, and gather hope into a soft place to rest when life grows hard and our spirit grows weary in the journey.
~L.R. Knost

IOWA KITCHEN TABLE WISDOM

YOU CAN'T GO HOME AGAIN

Beware of Destination Addiction—a preoccupation with the idea that happiness is in the next place, the next job or with the next partner. Until you give up the idea that happiness is somewhere else, it will never be where you are.
~Robert Holden, Ph.D

The title expression originated from Thomas Wolfe's novel *You Can't Go Home Again* published in 1940. The title of his book was inspired by a conversation with British journalist, Ella Winter, who remarked *"don't you know you can't go home again?"*

The book is about a successful writer who has published a novel about his family and hometown, exposing all of its flaws and blemishes. When he returns, he is met with outrage and hatred from family and friends.

A quote from Thomas Wolfe sums it up:

> *You can't go back home to your family, back home to your childhood, back home to romantic love, back home to a young man's dreams of glory and of fame...away from all the strife and conflict of the world...back home to someone who can help you, save you, ease the burden for you, back home to the old forms and systems of things which once seemed everlasting but which are changing all the time, back home to the escapes of time and memory.*

Deep and pervasive longings for a long ago time and place are easily triggered by a familiar song, an old photo, the smell of lilacs in the spring, a call from an old friend. Your recall of significant experiences, relationships, places, and other bits of the past, trigger positive emotions, yet a sense of loss.

Memories are far from perfect, and the memory bias effect doesn't help. Some forms of memory bias can be positive, protecting us from hurtful memories. Others can be negative, causing us to see the world as we expect to see it—even when we are wrong. Nostalgia of times and events of the past can seem wonderful and perfect, leading us to believe we can somehow recapture that perfect time.

Nostalgia is a powerful emotion. Political leaders throughout history have recognized this and have used it to manipulate voters into believing they can essentially turn back the clock.

Adolf Hitler promised to restore Germany to its former greatness. The phrase *"make Germany great again"* was a dominant theme in Nazi propaganda.

Ronald Reagan used the slogan *"Let's make America great again"* during his 1980 presidential campaign.

Margaret Thatcher, UK's Prime Minister during a general election address in 1950, stated her goal to *"make Britain great again."*

President of the Philippines, Ferdinand Marcos, promised that he could *"make this country great again."*

And, of course, more recently Donald Trump campaigned on the slogan *"Make America Great Again,"* suggesting that his policies and leadership could bring back the *"good ole days"* of the 50's, the reality of which was far from good for many people. It was a period of segregation and Jim Crow laws—a time when the nuclear family was the norm, one man, one woman, 2.5 children living in a whites-only suburban tract home—a time when women were supposed to marry, remain at home, cook and clean and raise the children, and married women could not obtain credit in their own name—a time when single women could not get birth control—a time when gays were still in the closet—a time of conformity and tradition. Everyone knew their role in society and were expected to act accordingly—and when they didn't the punishment could in some cases be death.

The President is also enamored by the idea of an economy fashioned after the Gilded Age, the 1870's, a period famous for blatant political corruption, with a deeply divided society of working class poor and "robber barons." A time when the rich got richer and the poor got poorer. It seems this one may be closer to becoming reality.

Through a kind of revisionist history—ignoring the reality of the problems of the past and the social, legal, and political changes that have occurred in subsequent years—political leaders will promise what common sense should tell you isn't going to happen. Yet, in the 2016 and 2024 elections millions of voters bought into the vision of restoring the Norman Rockwell/Gilded Age world that never was as perfect as the movies would have you believe.

We all occasionally long for a return to fondly recalled good times from the past. We think that if we can just recreate the situation, or go back to that location, or reconnect with the persons involved, we can relive those times and those feelings.

Unfortunately memories are just fragments—an incomplete picture of the past. Even the pieces that remain are flawed by an instinctual desire to make them more fun, exciting, and interesting than they actually were. Be thankful for the memories. Enjoying the old songs, reminiscing with old friends, remembering the fun times, watching old movies—this type of nostalgia is healthy. Longing for and attempting to live in the past can trigger depression and feeling of hopelessness.

By looking deeper into these memories, you may find that you wouldn't really want to return to the way it was. Life experiences—both good and bad— have helped shape who you are and defined your sense of self. Looking realistically at the past can help you realize how you've grown and how much you've gained since then. Instead of drawing comparisons between your life now and the memories of earlier times, be grateful for the defining life events and people who changed your life.

Making life decisions like relocating, changing jobs, getting divorced, etc. in an effort to recover a time long gone can be disastrous. Not only will it result in disappointment, but it can cause a sense of sadness and loss as the memory is destroyed by trying to recapture it. Time only moves in one direction—forward.

Treasure the memories of the past, but move on to make new memories. Go places you've never been, see things you've never seen, welcome new experiences, learn something new, meet new people and make new friends. Today's experiences will be tomorrow's memories. Make them good ones.

> *"You can have more than one home. You can carry your roots with you, and decide where they grow."*
> ~Henning Mankell

As Dorothy, in the *Wizard of Oz*, learned, although "home" may have changed, you can find it again where it's always been—in your heart.

YOU CAN'T GO HOME AGAIN

IOWA KITCHEN TABLE WISDOM

Nothing is Permanent Except Change

> *Change is the law of life. And those who look only to the past or the present are certain to miss the future*
> ~John F Kennedy

The title is from the Greek philosopher, Heraclitus, who was active around 500 BCE. He pointed out that everything is constantly shifting, regardless of what we do. He is best known for his "universal flux" doctrines that things are constantly changing, and that opposites coincide—things can be good and bad at the same time.

> *No man ever steps in the same river twice, for it's not the same river and he's not the same man.*
> ~Heraclitus

Whether you are an admirer of Heraclitus or have never heard of him, his philosophy speaks truth about the way the world works.

The spiritual writer Neale Donald Walsch describes change as follows:

> *Change is the shifting of any circumstance, situation, or condition, physical or nonphysical, in such a way that the original is rendered not merely different from what it was, but altered so radically as to make it utterly unrecognizable and impossible to return to anything resembling its former state.*

Whether we like it or not, change is a fact of life. Whether the change is coming from the outside and being forced upon you or whether it's a deliberate, purposeful, personal choice, it will still be stressful.

> *The secret of change is to focus your energy not fighting the old, but on building the new.*
>
> ~Socrates

A refusal to embrace change as a normal part of life will lead to fear, frustration, anger, and disappointment. How we handle change is the key to happiness—and even survival—particularly in our current world of uncertainty.

NOTHING IS PERMANENT EXCEPT CHANGE

It is not the strongest of the species that survive, nor the most intelligent, but the one most responsive to change.
~Charles Darwin

The climate is changing, creating record setting hurricanes and tornadoes. Melting glaciers are causing giant waves and rising sea levels that are reclaiming large land masses. Forests, a key line of defense against global warming around the world, are burning, from the Amazon to the Arctic, making sections of our planet uninhabitable.

Laws and rights we count on to protect us are no longer being recognized or enforced, as friends and neighbors are arrested and detained without charges or legal process. Our voting rights are under threat as gerrymandering, coercion, and extortion seem to be the new acceptable political tactic for gaining and holding power.

Life is change. Change is inevitable. However, when change is unpredictable and continuous, it can be quite frightening—even emotionally paralyzing. What to do, when to do it, what's coming next? How can we respond, much less prepare, for such an uncertain future?

While much is uncertain, there is something you can count on—things are NEVER going back to the way they were. The future we thought we would have is no longer even on our Bingo card! By accepting that the world we lived in less than a decade ago is gone—never to return—we can start to plan and adapt to "what is" rather than "what was" or "what we wish it was." Although life may never be the same again, that doesn't mean it can't be just as wonderful and fulfilling—in an entirely new and different way.

When we accept that our world has changed we're better able to plan and prepare. Once we quit dreading the future, we can start rebuilding our lives so we can adapt to whatever comes. The longer we wait, the harder it will be to adapt to the new situation. We can learn to thrive in change and uncertainty if we are prepared and flexible.

> *When the winds of change blow, some people build walls and others build windmills.*
> ~Chinese proverb

Having an open mind and a willingness to adapt are important characteristics for successfully dealing with new situations. Complacency is dangerous. Don't wait for change to happen. If we anticipate a change before it happens, we can avoid being forced into making reactive decisions that can end badly. Looking realistically at what

NOTHING IS PERMANENT EXCEPT CHANGE

"could" happen and having a plan if it does, makes the world a less frightening place. Initiating the change we want to see gives us more control over the outcome.

> *What comes, when it comes, will be what it is.*
> ~Alberto Caeiro

When life is uncertain, our ability to handle whatever comes depends on how prepared we are to "roll with the punches." If you make a list of the potential changes that are likely to impact you, your life, and your loved ones, you may be surprised to find the list is not as long as you thought. Much of what we worry about is not a direct or immediate threat to us or our way of life. We worry about what might happen because worrying gives us a sense of control in a situation we can't change.

> *Remember, today is the tomorrow you worried about yesterday.*
> ~Dale Carnegie

Accepting that things are likely to change can relieve some of the anxiety. Life gets easier when we stop fighting things we have no control over and just deal head-on with reality—the facts of life. A problem is something you can do something about. If you can't do anything about it, it's a fact of life. If you focus on solving the problems and learn to accept the facts of life, you will be happier and less stressed.

It's important to accept that things will likely be unsettling for a while, and it may be some time before you can be comfortable and feel safe again. When the future is unpredictable the message of the Serenity Prayer is particularly applicable:

> The Serenity Prayer
> *God grant me the serenity to accept the things I cannot change; the courage to change the things I can; and the wisdom to know the difference.*

Nothing is Permanent Except Change

IOWA KITCHEN TABLE WISDOM

Don't Believe Everything You Hear

There is no rest stop on the misinformation highway.
~Dahlia Lithwick
Journalist

We are living in a period that began in the mid to late 20th century known as "The Information Age." A time when we have unlimited and unprecedented access to information by just logging into our phone or computer.

Unfortunately, much of the information found online (and from televised news sources) is, at best, incorrect, incomplete, or biased, and often just plain false. The "Information Age" is also the "Misinformation/Disinformation Age."

Misinformation is everywhere. In a sense the news world has become like the high school rumor mill—filled with innuendos, false claims, and slanderous stories that get further from the truth with every telling—and the more outrageous, the better—more clicks, more viewers!

Fake news disguised as legitimate reporting can spread around the internet in minutes. Even more frightening is the rise of artificial intelligence (AI). Now we can't even believe what we see with our own eyes! We don't know what or who to believe.

> *Like it or not, we're still a primitive tribe ruled by fears, superstition and misinformation.*
> ~Bill Maher

Although the issue of misinformation has been around for centuries, the rapid rise of disinformation seems to have begun around the turn of the 21st century, beginning in the 1990's with the popularity and affordability of the home computer, followed shortly thereafter by smartphones with internet access and the launch of social media platforms like Friendster (2002), MySpace (2003), Facebook (2004), YouTube (2005), and Twitter (2006).

DON'T BELIEVE EVERYTHING YOU HEAR

Disinformation is not new. While information is power, disinformation is the abuse of power. It has always existed. In 1930s Germany it was known as propaganda. Hitler understood that if you repeat a lie often enough and convincingly state it, people will believe it. The purpose of political misinformation isn't just to promote a particular agenda, it's to exhaust the public trying to figure out what's true and what isn't.

The type of misinformation that is floating around the internet these days varies from information that is biased, misleading, or an outright lie with a goal of promoting a particular cause or point of view—to dangerous conspiracy theories that are designed to incite violence, and medical disinformation that can lead people to do things that are personally harmful to their health and can end up endangering the health of others.

So what can you do?

First, use your common sense. Does what you're reading or hearing sound logical? Lizard people? Jewish space lasers? A child sex trafficking ring in the basement of a pizza parlor? REALLY?

Second, determine the credibility of the source. Is this a legitimate news source, or have they been found to be a purveyor of "fake news" in the past, or like Fox News, been reclassified as "entertainment" vs "news"?

Third, ask yourself if the individual or news source might have a personal agenda, political bias, or something to gain either financially or politically by what they are claiming. If so, question the truthfulness of what they say.

Fourth, verify the information with reliable, independent, non-partisan sources like *PolitiFact.org; FactCheck.org;* or *Snopes.com.*

When it comes to information, whether from a news source, the internet, or from a friend or relative, a skeptical approach can be the prudent route to take.

> *Misinformation is not like a plumbing problem you fix. It is a social condition, like crime, that you must constantly monitor and adjust to.*
> ~Tom Rosenstiel
> Director of API

Don't Believe Everything You Hear

Commit Random Acts of Kindness

Do things for people not because of who they are or what they do in return, but because of who you are.
       ~Rabbi Harold Samuel Kushner

The title phrase is a shortened version. The earliest known appearance of the entire phrase was in a July 1985 article by Anne Herbert titled *"Random Kindness and Senseless Acts of Beauty"* published in the *Whole Earth Review*, an influential countercultural journal.

The phrase was picked up and repeated in various iterations by writers, celebrities, and political figures around the world, including comedian George Carlin and advice columnist Ann Landers. In 1958 *The Observer* newspaper of London published a radio drama that contained the phrase.

If you're tired of the anger, the hate, the fear, the division throughout the country, you're not alone. The majority of Americans say they are exhausted with the toxic divisiveness. Historians say this period is worse than it was during the Civil War.

> *I am loath to close. We are not enemies, but friends. We must not be enemies. Though passion may have strained, it must not break, our bonds of affection.*
> ~President Abraham Lincoln
> First Inaugural Address

The reality is that Democrats, Republicans, and Independents have something in common—we are all Americans. Despite having some strong differences on a number of issues, we are in this together. Unfortunately, we are not all rowing in the same direction!

Ben Franklin's words underscoring the importance of unity during the Revolutionary War, *"We must all hang together or we will all hang separately"* are relevant today when wars are breaking out around the world and, according to experts, the risk of a nuclear WW3 is the greatest it's been in decades.

Disagreements are to be expected. However, we can disagree without being disagreeable. There is a contagion of contempt, anger, and violence that is spreading like a virus for which there is apparently no vaccine. We all pay a steep price for our anger in terms of our physical and mental health.

We would like to think we have a corner on the truth. The reality is, the problems of this country and this world don't fit neatly into the diametrically opposing views of, *"Our side is right, and you guys are wrong."*

Connecting with others who have different ideas and beliefs is not easy, but they, like us, are doing the best they can to make sense out of the confusing and frightening world in which we live.

So what can we do? As the Glen Campbell song says we could *"Try a Little Kindness."*

Kindness is an alternative to violence and aggression, the repercussions of which can ripple out across communities, countries, and hopefully the world.

We are all "broken" in some way. We carry scars that cannot be seen. No one gets through life unscathed, but we all just do the best we can—just getting by with the help of our friends. You may never know the deep hurts of another person, and how much of a difference a small act of kindness can make in someone's life.

Have you ever done something nice for someone simply because you wanted to—with no expectations? Well, then, you've done a random act of kindness!

Being kind is beneficial to us as well as to the recipient of our kindness. Kind people are generally more likeable and have more friends. Kindness helps us build healthy relationships with others who, in return, will be more likely to protect and support us when we are in need. Kindness is contagious.

It's easy to be kind, but don't just be kind, be thoughtful. A kind person may be willing to give a helping hand when asked or when someone is obviously in need, but thoughtfulness goes beyond kindness. It means considering other people's feelings in our acts, words, and deeds and anticipating and responding to the needs and interests of others without being asked.

Thoughtfulness is a less common trait since it requires focusing on other people rather than on ourselves. A thoughtful action is a self-initiated action while a kind action is initiated by someone else.

One easy, thoughtful action is a sincere compliment. Complimenting a stranger for something they said, did, or just because you admire what they're wearing—can brighten their day. It's a sign of human empathy that will boost your sense of connection to humanity.

Thoughtfulness is the outward manifestation of compassion. Compassionate people feel other people's pain—they see not just the façade of life, they feel much deeper. They are what used to be called "soft hearted." These individuals are motivated to go out of their way to relieve the physical or emotional suffering of another—whether it's human or animal. It is a rare form of love that is triggered by true empathy—the active sharing and experiencing of another's pain. These are the ones like Mother Teresa who spent her life serving the poor; Martin Luther King, who gave his life for the cause of racial equality and justice; Oskar Shindler credited with saving the lives of 1,200 Jews during the German holocaust; and Harriet Tubman who risked her own life leading dozens of enslaved people to safety; Jane Goodall who redefined the traditional view that humans are uniquely different from other animals.

You don't need to give your life to express thoughtfulness and compassion. There are three little words that can make a difference in someone's life: *"Can I help?"*

IOWA KITCHEN TABLE WISDOM

JUDGE NOT, LEST YE BE JUDGED

> *Judge not, that ye be not judged. For with what judgment ye judge, ye shall be judged: and with what measure ye mete, it shall be measured to you. And why beholdest thou the mote that is in thy brother's eye, but considerest not the beam that is in thine own eye?*
> ~Matthew 7:1-3 (KJV)

This familiar quotation is from Christ's Sermon on the Mount. Most Christians (and even most non-Christians) have heard this spiritual directive, but are not necessarily inclined to apply it to themselves.

It's curious to note that those who consider themselves to be the most devout Christians, are often the quickest to judge the beliefs, behaviors, and life of others. When Christ taught, *"Judge not lest ye be judged,"* he was warning against the all too common human tendency to criticize and judge in order to feel superior—a type of spiritual hypocrisy. For many years, critics have bitterly denounced the hypocrisy in evangelical churches. In America today, faith plays a significant role in public and private life, and spiritual hypocrisy is rampant.

Many evangelical Christians truly believe that Trump's presidency reflects the will of God, some even declaring him to be their savior and that he was sent by God. For some voters, Trump and God are synonymous. History suggests that when his current actions and past behaviors are fully exposed (i.e. the Epstein files), the golden idol is destined to lose its shine and will crumble into dust, exposing the empty shell beneath.

> *Then the Lord said to Moses, "Go down, because your people, whom you brought up out of Egypt, have become corrupt. They have been quick to turn away from what I commanded them and have made themselves an idol cast in the shape of a calf. They have bowed down to it and sacrificed to it."*
> ~Exodus 32: 7-8 (NIV)

Those who advocate love, fidelity, truthfulness, and charity, but fail to live what they profess, are hypocrites. Often those that criticize others only reveal their own failings.

Jesus was teaching in the temple when the scribes and Pharisees, in an attempt to trap Jesus, brought a woman to him who had been caught in the act of adultery. They asked Jesus if she should be stoned as required by the Law of Moses. His response was:

> *"Let him who is without sin among you be the first to throw a stone at her."*
> ~John 8:7 (ESV)

From this passage Jesus made it clear that those who seek to judge others need to be more self-aware and examine their own shortcomings—search their own hearts and minds—before admonishing the actions of others.

There is nothing that hurts a relationship more than judgmental accusation. We know it hurts when it's done to us. So why would we continue to judge other people in the same way?

Judgmental thoughts are defensive reactions. The things we don't like about other people are often a reflection of our own issues or insecurities. Putting someone else down makes us feel better about ourselves—distracting us from our own shortcomings.

We can never fully understand someone else's circumstances. You don't know what you don't know. The well-known idiom *"walk a mile in his shoes"* carries a profound message urging us to recognize that we should not pass judgement if we've not experienced someone else's life challenges and struggles. Everyone has fears, hesitations, and baggage that are not always apparent.

One of the most common and dangerous actions we can take is passing judgement on others based on our own values, standards, and beliefs. We need to understand that no one hired us to monitor the choices others make. It's not our job to judge other people, and it's not our job to change other people—their life, their choices, or their beliefs.

> *Therefore you have no excuse, every one of you who judges. For in passing judgment on another you condemn yourself, because you, the judge, practice the very same things.*
> ~Romans 2 (ESV)

Creating a loving, accepting world starts with us, in both our thoughts and actions. The more we judge others, the less room we have for love.

JUDGE NOT LEST YE BE JUDGED

IOWA KITCHEN TABLE WISDOM

SOME PEOPLE DON'T WANT A SOLUTION

Someone with a victim mindset is always looking for a villain to blame and a situation to suffer from.
~Steve Maraboli
Author and Motivational Speaker

There may be people in your life that continually crave drama. They say and do things that ultimately turn into a disaster or create conflict. They love the attention. It's a form of addiction, and they will try to suck you into it. Because you care about them, your instinct will be to help—to give advice, money, shelter, a job—whatever.

If it happens once, it's a learning experience for both you and the individual. If it happens over and over, it's that person's lifestyle choice. These people need the type of help that is well beyond your paygrade.

The victim—we all know one—maybe you work with one, have a relative who is a victim, or maybe you are married to one—maybe you are one. The victim mentality can create a prison of self-pity, hindering personal growth and the ability to overcome challenges.

The victim believes they are helpless, powerless, and are constantly wronged by others. They will seek someone else to blame for situations they themselves have likely created. This is a mentality that works for them in order to avoid responsibility for their actions and the resulting negative outcomes. This is not a personality trait, it's a character flaw—a way of life that will not easily be dislodged!

> *You are not a product of your circumstances. You are a product of your decisions.*
> ~Stephen R. Covey

Some victims not only deny responsibility for their actions, but are continually on the lookout for someone to blame. One of the dangers is that when they run out of people to blame, don't be surprised if you end up becoming the target. These types are particularly toxic. They

SOME PEOPLE DON'T WANT A SOLUTION

manipulate and gaslight people around them. They cannot maintain relationships for any length of time because no one is perfect, and sooner or later every friend, every acquaintance, every family member will say or do something the victim takes offense at. The victim mentality is deeply engrained. Their victimhood is part of who they are. It has been perfected and has served them well. They've learned that being a victim has its benefits.

When dealing with a victim, nothing you say or do will fix their situation, because they don't really want it fixed. They may tell you all the tales of woe in their life, but will get angry if you offer a suggestion. They will just shut down or even blame you for suggesting they need help. They're not interested in solutions because if it's fixed they can no longer be a victim.

Trying to use logic or reason with a victim will not work. No matter how hard you try, they will refuse to do or change anything. They are determined to stay in their victimhood.

Listening to their endless tales of how they have been, or are being, mistreated can be exhausting. If you must, listen with empathy, but don't get sucked into the drama, don't take sides, and don't get emotional. You may feel guilty if you make an excuse to leave or change the subject, but you're not doing them any favors by encouraging them to wallow in their negativity.

When it's someone you care about, it's difficult to set boundaries—but for your own mental health, it's necessary. You're not being insensitive or rude or uncaring. You're doing what's best for you, and what's best for them, when you either excuse yourself or change the topic. It doesn't help to indulge them in their distorted view of reality and co-dependency.

So how do you know if you're dealing with someone just going through a bad time that needs your support vs a perpetual victim?

1. A victim is stuck in a never-ending cycle of self-pity. They will keep reliving and rehashing things that happened 10, 20, 30 or more years ago. They take pleasure in relating their story to anyone who will listen. If they were to let go and move on, they risk losing their best tool for manipulating and controlling others.

2. A victim has a history of blaming others for personal difficulties or failures rather than taking ownership and responsibility. They refuse to even try to control or address the problems in their life.

SOME PEOPLE DON'T WANT A SOLUTION

3. A victim seeks attention through pity or sympathy from others, constantly looking for validation by emphasizing their struggles and misfortunes.

4. A victim refuses help or advice, leading to isolation and rejection of the support that could help them grow and heal. Refusing help or advice can involve dismissing suggestions from friends or family, as well as avoiding professional guidance.

5. A victim typically leaves a long trail of broken relationships behind them, and you are likely to be added to that list because forgiveness is not part of their repertoire. Their motto is "one and done." If you are not properly attentive or if you unintentionally say or do something they find offensive—you're out. No second chances, no explanations! You will likely find yourself wondering "what the hell happened?"

6. A victim is a professional at holding grudges. They are unforgiving—trapped in a cycle of bitterness and resentment, preventing them from moving forward and experiencing emotional healing.

7. A victim with children is likely to be a "helicopter parent" trapping their children in a

world of fear, thwarting their emotional growth, and discouraging independence. It's likely the only long-term relationship they will have. That is, until the children realize what is happening and exercise their independence.

If the victim is someone close to you, it may be necessary to take a break from the relationship or even end it. There is no sense in trying to act or pretend like nothing unusual is going on. They are sick spiritually, physically, mentally, and emotionally, and will drain your energy and negatively impact your mental and emotional health.

The victim has likely been told by more than just a few people that they have problems, but until they were willing to face the truth, there is no convincing them to get help. Just like a drug addict won't give up his or her drug of choice until the consequences outweigh the benefits—a perpetual victim is not going to give up what has likely been working for them for years.

Save yourself and your sanity. You cannot live your best life dragging someone else's baggage along.

Some People Don't Want a Solution

IOWA KITCHEN TABLE WISDOM

You Can't Fix Stupid

"Sometimes a man wants to be stupid if it lets him do a thing his cleverness forbids."
~John Steinbeck

"You can't fix stupid" is a familiar American expression that pretty much everyone attributes to comedian Ron White who first popularized it in his stand-up act in 2005. Actually a variation of the phrase, "But I can't fix stupid," appeared much earlier than that in the comic strip *Shoe* by Jeff MacNelly on 4 August 1991. On 2 February 1995, Jim White (no relation to Ron White) was credited for it in the newspaper.

Regardless of who first coined the phrase, it's pretty self-explanatory. We have all met people who go through life believing stupid things or doing the same things over and over again and expecting different results—said to be the definition of insanity.

The word "STUPID" is defined as *"having or showing a great lack of intelligence or common sense; knowing or understanding something, but doing the wrong thing anyway."*

Ignorance and stupidity are not the same thing. I'm not stupid, but I (by choice) remain ignorant (unaware) of the goings-on of any of the Kardashians!

We all know someone who laments that people treat them like they're stupid. They keep saying and doing stupid things and refuse to consider the possibility they could be wrong. They don't know what they're talking about, yet they won't stop talking!

When you meet a stupid person, realize that not only can you not fix stupid—you can't argue with stupid. Some people choose to remain uninformed and won't listen to anyone else. These are the same people who believe their opinion outweighs facts and reality. They will not be moved by facts or change their opinion even when faced with indisputable reality.

It's amazing how many examples of people saying stupid things can be found on the internet. These individuals are an example of what you get with a

You Can't Fix Stupid

failing educational system. Here are some **ACTUAL** quotes that appeared on various social media sites:

> "My sister is pregnant. I can't wait to see if imma be an aunt or an uncle."

> "Don't you find it stupid that Obama is the only president without a last name?"

> "Why does the woman never have to take a DNA test to see if it's their child?"

> "If Biden wins I'm leaving the US and going to Hawaii!!"

> "That's it. That seals the deal. I've been an American citizen for 54 years and in all my time of being one I've never seen an election this bad. I've had enough of it. Until you fix this country, I'll be packing my bags to Alaska where they actually know how to run a country."

> "We don't need farmers because we have grocery stores." (Yes, this is a real posting!)

> "Windmills cool down the Earth to stop global warming."

> "Dear Atheists: How is it that cave men survived the asteroid but the dinosaurs didn't?" (They stayed 65 million years apart???)

"You shouldn't drink carbonated water; it's full of carbs!"

"Space was created by Disney to further the hoax of the earth being round." (HUH???)

"Is there any sort of book subscription for kids that exists where you order books and once you read them you return them and get more?" (A library???)

"Wow. I can't believe America is 2020 years old today. Happy 4th of July."

"How did people in the Middle Ages know what skeletons looked like without X-ray machines?" (Ummm...dead people?)

"I swear, someone needs to invent socks for our hands. My hands are always cold." (Ever heard of gloves or mittens?)

"Mount Everest is in the United States. It's where those four white guys are carved into the rock." (Ummm...that's Mount Rushmore and the "four white guys" are U.S. Presidents—2nd grade history!)

Stupid people—we can't avoid them, so how do we deal with them?

It's hard to win an argument with a smart person, but it's near impossible to win an argument with a stupid person. When you know you're going to be dealing with a stupid person, avoid bringing up any subject that might challenge anything they believe. Stick to the safe subjects—which for some people is a limited list, especially these days when even talking about the weather can be a trigger!

If the stupid person brings up a controversial subject and begins to hold forth on something you know is not just wrong, but ridiculous, resist the urge to jump in and give them the facts. They don't want the facts. They want you to accept their opinion. Be as nice as you can (pretend you are dealing with a small child who believes in Santa Claus or the Easter Bunny). This behavior will disarm and possibly confuse them, leaving them little choice but to shut up since they have no one to argue with. Then change the subject or excuse yourself. Remember, silence is an argument won by other means. Having an urgent need to use the restroom is always a good ploy for excusing yourself.

Just remember that if this person is an adult and no one has been able to "fix" them so far, you're no more likely than the rest to succeed. Just smile to yourself and repeat in your head *"You Can't Fix Stupid."*

IOWA KITCHEN TABLE WISDOM

TAKE THE HIGH ROAD

If you have integrity, nothing else matters. If you don't have integrity, nothing else matters.
                    ~Alan Simpson

The author of the above quotation, Alan Simpson, was a Republican politician from Wyoming. He was a political legend whose quick wit bridged partisan gaps during the years when the party still valued ethics and integrity.

The phrase "take the high road" is a common English expression that has been used for centuries. One possible explanation for a source comes from an old proverb:

The high road leads to heaven, but the low road leads to hell.

It refers to taking the moral or ethical path, rather than choosing an easier or more personally beneficial option. It has its roots in Scottish history, where it was originally used to refer to a main thoroughfare that was elevated above surrounding terrain and less traveled.

Over time, this phrase evolved beyond its literal meaning and began to be used figuratively in everyday speech. Today, the quotation implies that doing the right thing, even when it's not easy, obvious, or popular, shows maturity and integrity. Having a reputation for doing what is right often leads to better long-term outcomes and stronger, more lasting relationships.

The idea of taking the high road is associated with people who are honored and respected. Choosing to take the high road can demonstrate strength of character and an unimpeachable commitment to doing what is right in every situation.

The concept of taking the high road is prevalent in cultures around the world, although it may not be expressed in those words. In Western culture, it's associated with being honest and fair in business and in personal relationships. In Eastern cultures such as Japan and China, there is an emphasis on saving face and avoiding confrontation by choosing a peaceful resolution instead of engaging in conflict.

It's important to understand that not all situations have a clear-cut high road. Sometimes it's subjective and depends on individual values and beliefs—personal ethics.

Personal ethics are principles we use when making decisions. Personal ethics are your guidelines for relationships, dealing with challenges, and decision-making. They are based on experience, opinion, and perspective and on what you believe to be ethical behavior. Personal ethics covers your personal beliefs about honesty, loyalty, integrity, respect and responsibility.

Whether you realize it or not, you use your personal ethics regularly, and when you violate them, it can negatively affect your mood, your mental health, your relationships, and even your personal freedom. At the very least, it will cause guilt and shame from knowing what you said or did. Even if it's never discovered, you will carry the guilt and it will affect your life and happiness.

Some situations may require navigating a "gray area," where it's unclear what's right and what's wrong. It's important to have a clear view in your own mind of what your personal ethics will allow and not allow. Whether those ethics stem from a religious upbringing or something you have adopted through experience along the way, being firm about what is, and is not, okay will make life a lot easier.

> *Every time we turn our heads the other way when we see the law flouted, when we tolerate what we know to be wrong, when we close our eyes and ears to the corrupt because we are too busy or too frightened, when we fail to speak up and speak out, we strike a blow against freedom, decency, and justice.*
> ~Robert F. Kennedy

We need to be clear what we stand for—what we will fight for, what we will fight against.

> *Living with integrity means: Not settling for less than what you know you deserve in your relationships. Asking for what you want and need from others. Speaking your truth, even though it might create conflict or tension. Behaving in ways that are in harmony with your personal values. Making choices based on what you believe, and not what others believe.*
> ~Barbara De Angelis
> Consultant and lecturer

Instead of engaging in a heated argument (which you will never win), choosing to "take the high

Take the High Road

road" and walk away is a better option.

While taking the high road may not always lead to an obvious immediate reward, it can build trust and credibility. The short term gains of unethical behavior may immediately pay off, but will likely not end well and can destroy relationships, careers, reputation, and your mental health.

IOWA KITCHEN TABLE WISDOM

Embrace the Uncertainty

I can live with doubt and uncertainty and not knowing. I think it is much more interesting to live not knowing than to have answers that might be wrong. If we will only allow that, as we progress, we remain unsure, we will leave opportunities for alternatives. We will not become enthusiastic for the fact, the knowledge, the absolute truth of the day, but remain always uncertain. In order to make progress, one must leave the door to the unknown ajar.
~Richard P. Feynman

The above quotation is by Richard Phillips Feynman, an American theoretical physicist and Nobel laureate who made groundbreaking contributions to quantum mechanics, quantum electrodynamics (QED), and particle physics. Although the quote applies to the field of science and the search for answers about the universe and it's structure, it certainly is relevant to the times we are living in—a time of critical uncertainty about everything. Our lives, our country, and our world are going through a major transition period. It is unlike any other period known to man. Each day there is another challenge to the status quo.

Sometimes it feels as though everything's falling apart. We can only guess at what the future will look like—much less make plans or prepare for what is to come. The world is spinning out of control and no longer seems to make sense. If you focus on what's wrong with the world, you are likely to (justifiably) feel afraid, paralyzed, helpless, and full of rage. Life doesn't seem fair, kind, right, or even real anymore. You long to escape, but there is no escape hatch!

So what do we do? We have no choice. If we are to survive with some sense of sanity, we must learn how to lean in and embrace the unknown—the uncertain future—to honor the scary place of not knowing.

If you are overcome by trying to control, or make sense of everything—STOP. Stop pushing for answers. Questions will get answered or not answered, and solutions will appear or not

EMBRACE THE UNCERTAINTY

appear—things will get better or things will get worse. It is all out of your control. The sooner you acknowledge this, the sooner you will be able to settle into not knowing—letting go of how life was before and what you had planned for the future.

Trust the place where you are now and make choices and decisions based on what is—not what was or what you think it will, or should, be. The future is unstable ground that can change in an instant. Love the place where you are now, love the ground upon which you stand in this instant. This is the ground from which your new life will grow. Focusing on the past and the future disconnects you from where you are now. Be present in your life as it is. Any necessary decision will make itself in time.

Since there is no other choice than to be where you are, consider using this as a period of re-assessment. Acknowledge the reality, but don't use it as an excuse to give up.

Stop and take a deep breath. Consider that this is exactly how things are supposed to be right now. Let go, and relax into uncertainty, not knowing what the next step will be, but knowing that whatever happens, you will get through it. You will survive and adjust to whatever the new reality serves up.

It's normal to desire certainty, but understand that everything except this very moment is uncertain. It's always been that way. It's just that there is so much chaos and change in the world right now, uncertainty has risen to the top of our awareness! Most people don't acknowledge all of the uncertainties that exist even in normal times. You don't know what will happen in a month, a year—you don't even know what will happen tomorrow. You can waste a lot of time, stress, and energy trying to guess about an uncertain future.

You want to feel prepared. The problem is, no one can know the future before it happens. Learning to tolerate the discomfort of uncertainty means standing aside and seeing how the future actually unfolds and dealing with it once it's here. Trust that the future will come, and you'll deal with whatever it holds when you get there. In the meantime, live life like an adventure.

> *Life is about not knowing, having to change, taking the moment and making the best of it, without knowing what's going to happen next. Delicious Ambiguity.*
> ~Gilda Radner

EMBRACE THE UNCERTAINTY

IOWA KITCHEN TABLE WISDOM

LIFE BEGINS AT THE END OF YOUR COMFORT ZONE

Consider who is the happier man—he who has braved the storm of life and lived or he who has stayed securely on shore and merely existed?
                              ~Hunter S. Thompson

The title is by Neale Donald Walsch, the author of 40 books on spirituality and its practical application in everyday life, whose words have had a profound affect around the world. His most well-known is a series known as *Conversations with God* from which the title quote was taken.

It takes courage to face the unknown—the unfamiliar. We fear what we don't know.

Being stuck in a repetitive life is not the proper way to live. We never know how much time we have so we need to make the most of it. Push yourself to do something you wouldn't normally do, and venture beyond your comfort zone because that is where life truly does begin. You will achieve things you never knew you were capable of. You will discover new interests, new friends and new facets of life by breaking away from your repetitive, safe life and venturing beyond your comfort zone.

Too much reliance on staying within a comfort zone can become a prison—fears can develop into phobias—creating a prison without walls or bars. It's scary, and sometimes we need to be pushed across the line. The greatest barrier to success and happiness is fear, and facing that fear head on is the doorway to truly living.

Whether it's fear of failure, embarrassment, criticism, fear of being ridiculed or laughed at, financial fears, fear of sin or hell, illness or injury—whatever—life is too short and precious to spend it in terror of things that may never happen. If you live your life in persistent fear, clutching at the status quo in white-knuckled desperation, you are missing the joy that life has to offer. Just on the other side of your comfort zone is a full and exciting life.

LIFE BEGINS AT THE END OF YOUR COMFORT ZONE

> *My experience is that you cannot have everything you want, but you can have anything you really want. You just need to decide what it is and then plan your exit from the comfort zone.*
> ~Jonathan Farrington

The comfort zone consists of regular and familiar behaviors, routines, and actions where there are low levels of stress and anxiety with little-to-no risk. It's secure and you feel in control—you know what to expect. Your life may be full of opportunities, but seizing them can be a real challenge if you don't leave your comfort zone.

Our comfort zone is a type of security blanket—like Linus in the *Peanuts* comic strip. We believe it gives us security, but this is an illusion giving no more safety than Linus' blanket.

Live your life so that when the end comes, you have no bucket list, having done all of the things you wanted to do, and have no regrets.

> *Life is not a journey to the grave with the intention of arriving safely in a pretty and well preserved body, but rather to skid in broadside, thoroughly used up, totally worn out, and loudly proclaiming —WOW—What a Ride!*
> ~Unknown

IOWA KITCHEN TABLE WISDOM

STOP AND SMELL THE ROSES

When you bring your attention to a stone, a tree or an animal, something of its essence transmits itself to you. You can sense how still it is and in doing so the same stillness rises within you. You can sense how deeply it rests in being completely one with what it is and where it is, in realizing this, you too come to a place of rest deep within yourself.
~Eckhart Tolle

The title is a variation of a saying generally attributed to Walter Hagen, a famous golfer and author of an autobiography, *The Walter Hagen Story* in which he said, *"You're only here for a short visit. Don't hurry. Don't worry. And be sure to smell the flowers along the way."* The quote became famous in different variations—*"stop and smell the flowers"* and *"stop and smell the roses."* In 1974, singer Mac Davis hit the top 10 on the charts with his *"Stop and Smell the Roses." "Stop and Smell the Roses"* was also the name of a 1981 solo album by Beatles drummer, Ringo Starr.

The saying is an admonition to slow down and truly be present in the moment—finding joy in the world around you.

Stress can kill you. Turn on the morning news, open your local newspaper, or check your emails and it will raise your blood pressure, create anxiety, and cause serious depression. There doesn't seem to ever be good news anymore. The world is filled with hate, anger, and violence—neighbor vs neighbor; liberal vs conservative; Christian vs Muslim—with threats of war, threats to freedom, threats to individuals—armed troops in American cities, businesses closing, dire economic, job, and healthcare predictions; and global warming destroying entire communities with wildfires, tornadoes, hurricanes, floods, and earthquakes. There doesn't seem to be anything hopeful or optimistic to look forward to—just more of the same. It's easy to be distressed, discouraged, and yes—exhausted. Finding a place and a time to unwind, breathe, and heal has never been more critical!

Seeking solace in nature has become increasingly important to our physical and mental health, and our emotional well-being. Spending time in natural surroundings can heal our hearts and our minds and restore balance in our lives. There's something about being surrounded by nature that soothes the soul, calms the mind and lifts the spirit. Science has shown that nature is a powerful antidote to stress and anxiety, promoting mental and emotional well-being.

> *I don't have any idea of who or what God is. But I do believe in some great spiritual power. I feel it particularly when I'm out in nature. It's just something that's bigger and stronger than what I am or what anybody is. I feel it. And it's enough for me.*
> ~Jane Goodall
> Anthropologist

You don't need to retreat from the world to experience the benefits of communing with nature. Immersing oneself in the wonders of nature is a powerful and easily attainable form of healing. The easiest way to find inner peace in nature is to be in it!

> *There is a pleasure in the pathless woods,*
> *There is a rapture on the lonely shore,*
> *There is society where none intrudes,*
> *By the deep sea, and music in its roar.*
> *I love not man the less but nature more.*
> ~Lord Byron

Take a moment to sit outside, close your eyes, take a deep breath and let your senses take everything in—the warmth of the sun, the birds calling to each other, the smell of an early morning rain on the earth. Being present in nature helps us feel connected to one another and appreciate the magic of our natural world.

> *A human being is part of a whole, called by us the 'Universe' —a part limited in time and space. He experiences himself, his thoughts, and feelings, as something separated from the rest—a kind of optical delusion of his consciousness. This delusion is a kind of prison for us, restricting us to our personal desires and to affection for a few persons nearest us. Our task must be to free ourselves from this prison by widening our circles of compassion to embrace all living creatures and the whole of nature in its beauty.*
> ~Albert Einstein

When you're feeling overwhelmed, distressed, exhausted, or discouraged, take a time out. When you are in beautiful, peaceful settings, your eyes and mind are distracted from day to day issues that dominate your thoughts.

Fortunately, nature doesn't have rules or time requirements. It allows us to just be present.

STOP AND SMELL THE ROSES

Whether you prefer the sound of wind in the trees, the sight of sunlight dancing on the water, or the smell of blooming jasmine, spending time in the natural world reduces stress, improves mood, and even boosts the immune system.

> *The kiss of the sun for pardon, The song of the birds for mirth, One is nearer God's heart in a garden Than anywhere else on earth.*
> ~Dorothy Frances Gurney
> *God's Garden*

So let nature's beauty work its magic to help you develop a deeper connection to yourself, and to the Universe around you. Nature is a powerful force for healing the body, mind, and spirit, reminding us of our connection to all living things.

> *I love Nature partly because she is not man, but a retreat from him. None of his institutions control or pervade her. There a different kind of right prevails. In her midst I can be glad with an entire gladness. If this world were all man, I could not stretch myself, I should lose all hope. He is constraint, she is freedom to me. He makes me wish for another world. She makes me content with this one.*
> ~Henry David Thoreau
> *Journal*, 3 January 1853

IOWA KITCHEN TABLE WISDOM

No Good Deed Goes Unpunished

The expression "no good deed goes unpunished" has often been attributed to Clare Boothe Luce, but the attribution was weak because the phrase had been circulating for multiple years before.

It actually originates from the 12th century work of author Walter Map, *De nugis curialium* (Medieval Latin for *"Of the trifles of courtiers"* or loosely *"Trinkets for the Court"*). The book takes the form of a series of anecdotes of people and places, offering many sidelights on the history of his own time.

The following poem by newspaper columnist Franklin Pierce Adams (1881-1960), is entitled *"No Good Deed Goes Unpunished"* and illustrates the potential for unintended consequences from good intentions.

There was a man in our town who had King Midas' touch; He gave away his millions to the colleges and such;

And people cried: "The hypocrite! He ought to understand the ones who really need him are the children of this land!"

When Andrew Croesus built a home for children who were sick, the people said they rather thought he did it as a trick.

And writers said: "He thinks about the drooping girls and boys, but what about conditions with the men whom he employs?"

There was a man in our town who said that he would share, his profits with his laborers, for that was only fair.

And people said: "Oh, isn't he the shrewd and foxy gent? It cost him next to nothing for that free advértisement!"

There was a man in our town who had the perfect plan, to do away with poverty and other ills of man.

But he feared the public jeering, and the folks who would defame him, so he never told the plan he had, and I can hardly blame him.

Helping others, in small and large ways, is what the good book tells you to do. Doing good deeds is stimulating and satisfying. It helps you feel socially connected, which is good for your happiness and health. In fact a recent study published in the journal *Proceedings of the National Academy of Sciences of the USA* shows that doing a good deed not only helps the recipient, but brings the giver physical pleasure and pain relief. Authors in the study concluded "*Acting altruistically relieved not only acutely induced physical pain among healthy adults but also chronic pain among cancer patients.*"

> *You cannot do kindness too soon, for you never know how soon it will be too late.*
> ~Ralph Waldo Emerson

Some people don't want help—and they may even seek to punish you for your efforts. There are some situations when people are uncomfortable with being helped, and may even become hostile if you try. Just about everyone has at some time noticed someone who seems to be suffering and inquired "is there something wrong?" only to be told "mind your own business."

You may have had friends ask for your advice when they were having a bad time, and after you told them what you thought would help, they turned on you—because they didn't want to hear that THEY needed to change or do something they didn't want to do.

If you don't want to be hurt when your intentions were good, be careful who and how you help.

It is a sad world indeed when a well-intentioned act of kindness cannot go undisturbed by petty criticism or hateful words fueled by ignorance.
~B Devine
Songwriter, poet

While it's not true that "NO good deed goes unpunished," it can occasionally backfire.

I don't regret the things I did wrong, I regret the good things I did for the wrong people.
~Cameron Mattox

No Good Deed Goes Unpunished

IOWA KITCHEN TABLE WISDOM

The Universe is Unfolding As It Should

The title of this essay is the phrase that begins the final paragraph in the 1927 poem *Desiderata,* a poem that was especially popular in the 1960's but continues to be quoted today. The title is Latin for "things deserved."

There was a legend that it had been found on an old piece of parchment in St Paul's Church in Baltimore and that the poem itself dated from the late 1600s. But that was not the case. It was actually written by Max Ehrmann (1872-1945), an American writer, poet, and attorney from Indiana who often wrote on spiritual themes. The poem is now within the public domain and is available printed and framed on multiple internet sites.

It has commonly been misinterpreted as a strongly nihilistic philosophy posing the concept that nothing can be done about your lot in life--that life has no intrinsic worth, purpose, or order, so just surrender—reminiscent of the line "Resistance is futile" as uttered by the evil Borg robotic aliens in the third-season finale of *Star Trek: The Next Generation.*

In reality, it is not that at all. In fact, in the 1960s, it found a following among the San Francisco flower children, who embraced it as an affirmation of love, hope, and peace—an inspiration for making the world a better place.

It is NOT, as many others who are only familiar with that singular line suggest, a call to ignore the cruelty and inequality in the world because *"the universe is unfolding as it should."* Nor does it suggest that you should turn your back on those who need help.

It does NOT advocate becoming a "doomsday prepper" or isolationist, or otherwise withdrawing from the larger family, community, or political responsibilities.

It contains many excellent pieces of wisdom for living a fulfilling and independent life. Each line carries a deep and thoughtful message. Every

The Universe Is Unfolding As It Should

time you read it you will likely find something new. Following is the original as it was first published.

> *Go placidly amid the noise and the haste, and remember what peace there may be in silence.*
>
> *As far as possible, without surrender, be on good terms with all persons. Speak your truth quietly and clearly; and listen to others, even to the dull and the ignorant; they too have their story.*
>
> *Avoid loud and aggressive persons; they are vexatious to the spirit.*
>
> *If you compare yourself with others, you may become vain or bitter, for always there will be greater and lesser persons than yourself.*
>
> *Enjoy your achievements as well as your plans. Keep interested in your own career, however humble; it is a real possession in the changing fortunes of time.*
>
> *Exercise caution in your business affairs, for the world is full of trickery. But let this not blind you to what virtue there is; many persons strive for high ideals, and everywhere life is full of heroism.*

Iowa Kitchen Table Wisdom

Be yourself. Especially do not feign affection. Neither be cynical about love; for in the face of all aridity and disenchantment, it is as perennial as the grass.

Take kindly the counsel of the years, gracefully surrendering the things of youth.

Nurture strength of spirit to shield you in sudden misfortune. But do not distress yourself with dark imaginings. Many fears are born of fatigue and loneliness.

Beyond a wholesome discipline, be gentle with yourself. You are a child of the universe no less than the trees and the stars; you have a right to be here.

And whether or not it is clear to you, no doubt the universe is unfolding as it should. Therefore be at peace with God, whatever you conceive Him to be.

And whatever your labors and aspirations, in the noisy confusion of life, keep peace in your soul. With all its sham, drudgery and broken dreams, it is still a beautiful world. Be cheerful. Strive to be happy.
~Max Ehrmann

THE UNIVERSE IS UNFOLDING AS IT SHOULD

IOWA KITCHEN TABLE WISDOM

NOT MY CIRCUS, NOT MY MONKEYS

"No is a complete sentence. It does not require an explanation to follow."
~ Sharon E. Rainey

"Not my circus. Not my monkeys" is an old Polish proverb referring to a situation that isn't your problem. Some people have adopted this philosophy as a reminder to not get involved with things that don't involve them.

It's easy to find ourselves caught up in other people's issues. A friend calls about problems at work. Your adult child is having problems with their spouse and asks your advice or asks you to intervene. Your neighbor is being evicted and needs money. Your drug-addicted nephew needs a place to crash.

You are a caring, compassionate person—a good

Christian. You want to be a good neighbor, a good friend, a good Samaritan, but you've found that in the past, it often does not end well for you. Maybe the advice you gave your friend ended up getting her fired. You find yourself being blamed for "interfering" in your adult child's marriage. You made a loan to your neighbor and now they've left town and your money is never repaid. Your nephew snuck away in the middle of the night with your great-grandmother's antique diamond ring.

We all, if we are normal, struggle with the word "no." We don't want to appear rude or uncaring, so we often end up the ringmaster in someone else's circus!

Learning to say no and to set healthy boundaries helps us take control of our lives, so we're not constantly being taken advantage of or getting ourselves caught up in situations that make us vulnerable to abuse.

Saying no isn't selfish or unkind. It's declaring that our time, energy, and mental health is important.

Declaring *"Not my circus. Not my monkeys"* is a way of making it clear that something isn't your responsibility. It's an appropriate response when a situation or problem is beyond your control or doesn't actually involve you.

One example is when friends, family, or co-workers try to pull you into their drama wanting you to take a side in a conflict that has nothing to do with you. The danger here is that if you get involved, it can backfire, and you could end up getting blamed for the outcome.

On the other hand, it's important to find a balance between not getting involved and recognizing when you do have the control (and the responsibility) to deal with something. You can't just ignore situations where someone is in actual danger.

One example where you may want to get involved is when you're unhappy with the current political situation. It is your civic duty to participate—it is your circus AND your monkeys when the result of an election may directly affect you or your family.

You may find yourself in a situation where you recognize that you aren't responsible and probably shouldn't get involved, but you still feel compelled to do something. This usually happens when it involves someone you care about. Before making a decision, ask yourself how getting involved might make you feel, and more importantly, <u>would it actually fix the problem</u>.

When you find yourself facing a situation where you're being pressured to get involved and you know it is not your circus or your monkeys, how do you extricate yourself politely?

Using the actual phrase is often appropriate. However, used in a personal situation it may imply that you don't care about another person's problems. In that case, you can say the same thing in other ways. Here are a few alternatives:

> "I'm sorry you're going through this. I hope you can find a resolution."

> "You know I care for you and wish you the best, but I really can't get involved."

> "I'm sorry to hear about your family problems. Stay strong. I'm sure you will figure it out."

Remember, saying "no" is a powerful tool that allows you to take control of your life and make choices to protect your mental health, safety, and priorities.

NOT MY CIRCUS, NOT MY MONKEYS

IOWA KITCHEN TABLE WISDOM

When People Walk Away, Let Them

When people walk away from you, let them go. Your destiny is never tied to anyone who leaves you, and it doesn't mean they are bad people. It just means that their part in your story is over.
~T. D. Jakes

The title and quotation originated with megachurch pastor, Thomas Dexter Jakes, Sr. an American Christian pastor, motivational speaker, and author.

Goodbyes mark the transition of something—the ending of one thing and the beginning of another. Some goodbyes are difficult and painful. Some can be healing and helpful. Saying goodbye doesn't mean we hate someone. It means their presence in our life has become more painful than helpful. We are often saying goodbye to toxicity and emotional injury. We are no longer willing to subject ourselves to abuse from others. Life will go on and wonderful things will happen. Learning to say goodbye can be a healthy thing.

Your future is not about people who walk away. It's about people who stay. People come into your life for a reason, a season, or a lifetime. Accept people as they are, but place them where they belong. When they leave, it's because your paths are not the same. Mourn them if you must, but accept the reality that your lessons are different.

Every relationship serves a purpose. Then, without any wrongdoing on your part, this person may say or do something to bring the relationship to an end. Buddha taught that not every person is meant to stay in your life. True strength and freedom lies in letting go—of people, situations, and attachments that disturb your inner peace.

When someone is in your life for a REASON, it is usually to meet a current need you have. They are there for the reason you need them to be. These people will influence your decisions, help you through the bad times, share your sorrows and your joys, but at some point they may no longer be part of your life. You are not the center of the universe for anyone's life except your own. You must accept when it's time for you or them to move on.

> *Life is too short to leave the key to your happiness in someone else's pocket.*
> ~Unknown

Some people come into your life for a SEASON, to share, grow or learn. They bring you an experience. They may teach you something. They usually give you an unbelievable amount of joy. It is real—but only for a season. Some people need to leave our lives for their own reasons. When it's time for them to go, let them go. Sometimes you just have to recognize that you were the only one trying to make things work.

A very few people are in your life for a LIFETIME. Lifetime relationships can come into your life at any point, but they will be there until the end. Lifetime relationships teach lifetime lessons—things you can build on in order to have a solid emotional foundation. Your job is to accept the lessons, love the person, and put what you have learned to use in all other relationships and areas of your life. Honor and cherish a lifetime relationship.

Give back to them what they have given to you—loyalty, honesty, love, and support—and never take them for granted.

> *There comes a point in your life when you realize who matters, who never did, who won't anymore, and who always will. So, don't worry about people from your past, there's a reason why they didn't make it to your future.*
> ~Adam Lindsay Gordon

When people drift away, let them go with love. The ones meant to stay will always find their way back. You need to let some people go, not because you don't care, but because they don't.

> *I'm just thankful for the people that never left me and equally thankful for those who did.*
> ~Nitya Prakash

WHEN PEOPLE WALK AWAY, LET THEM

IOWA KITCHEN TABLE WISDOM

BE YOURSELF, EVERYONE ELSE IS TAKEN

The highest courage is to dare to be yourself in the face of adversity. Choosing right over wrong, ethics over convenience, and truth over popularity— these are choices that measure your life. Travel the path of integrity without looking back, for there is never a wrong time to do the right thing.

~Michael Moore

The earliest compelling match for this phrase appeared in 1967 in the literary journal *The Hudson Review* in an essay by Thomas Merton. Thomas Merton was a spiritual thinker and mystic. In his essay *Day of a Stranger*, he humorously stated *"In an age where there is much talk about 'being yourself,' I reserve to myself the right to forget about being myself, since in any case there is very little chance of my being anybody else."* Regardless of the origin of the saying, it is a clever and witty way to express the importance of living an authentic life—being true to yourself.

Living your authentic self regardless of the situation or the audience can often be difficult. Those who live authentically must learn to stand in their truth in the face of adversity. There is no shortage of people who think they know what's best for you—who will be happy to tell you how to live, what to believe, how to act, who to love, etc. It requires courage to stand up for who you are amidst criticism and even threats from friends or loved ones. It means refusing to bow to pressure to be someone you're not in order to fit into a mold that society, your family or friends have created.

> *To be yourself in a world that is constantly trying to make you something else is the greatest accomplishment.*
> ~Ralph Waldo Emerson

Authentic living requires a clear moral compass driven by the principles of honesty, respect, humility, compassion, courage, and accountability. It's about making the choice every day to embody these values, even when it's hard.

BE YOURSELF, EVERYONE ELSE IS TAKEN

The reality is, courage isn't about being fearless, but about taking action despite our fears.

Authentic living is a courageous and even a spiritual act requiring the strength to insist on respect, not just for yourself, but for all individuals, regardless of their status or background—treating everyone with kindness, dignity, and compassion—understanding that everyone has their own story and journey with their own battles and challenges.

When you are living your authentic life, your actions are guided by truth and purpose—removing all emotional blocks and limiting beliefs. It means embracing your strengths, acknowledging your weaknesses, and striving to be the best version of the authentic you—rejecting the pressure to please others or conform to societal expectations. It means expressing your genuine thoughts and feelings, even amidst opposition and conflict, free of restrictions about who you can be, what you can do, and what you should believe.

Unfortunately, there will always be those who try to dissuade you, discourage you, or even lie about you. They may seek to undermine your personal growth because of their own fears or selfish needs. When you don't do what they want, they may deliberately set out to hurt you. Nothing cuts quite as deep as deception from people you care about. It can shake you to your core and make you question your truth. The healthiest thing you can do is not respond, ignore the lies, and rise above the drama. This type of individual has problems that have nothing to do with you.

It's been said that people may shape us or try to break us, but in the end they make us who we are.

> *The ultimate measure of a man is not where he stands in moments of comfort and convenience, but where he stands at times of challenge and controversy.*
> ~Martin Luther King, Jr.

BE YOURSELF, EVERYONE ELSE IS TAKEN

IOWA KITCHEN TABLE WISDOM

PROTECT YOUR BOUNDARIES

Love yourself enough to set boundaries. Your time and energy are precious. You get to choose how you use it. You teach people how to treat you by deciding what you will and won't accept.
~Anna Taylor

A personal boundary expresses where your responsibilities or space begins and other people's end. Healthy boundaries define what is appropriate behavior in a relationship. Boundaries are essential for our overall mental health and well-being. Boundaries establish how you are to be treated and how you are willing to spend your time, energy and money.

You may fear that boundaries will push people away, but those who truly care will respect your limits. Maturity is learning to establish boundaries with people and situations that threaten your peace of mind, self-respect, values, morals and self-worth. Boundaries are the bridges that keep relationships balanced. A boundary is not rejection. It is expressing your needs clearly and without apology. Setting expectations for yourself and others is a way of claiming your life and time, and learning to say no without guilt. It's teaching others how to treat you.

Having healthy boundaries involves focusing on what is yours to control and insisting that others respect your decisions. It means taking responsibility for your own thoughts and actions, and letting other people take responsibility for their thoughts and actions. For some people that's a hard lesson to learn.

Boundary issues often come disguised as conflict. After years of not establishing personal boundaries, when you finally decide "enough is enough" you will likely experience some personal guilt. The decision may cause surprise, and possibly anger, from those who have been taking advantage of or mistreating you.

> *If someone throws a fit because you set boundaries, it's just more evidence that boundaries were needed.*
> ~Unknown

PROTECT YOUR BOUNDARIES

Family situations are the most challenging for setting boundaries, and the most likely to cause personal guilt. It's not your job to fix people. It's not your job to save people whose life is out of control—although you may get the blame.

It isn't easy to set limits, especially with people you love, but your personal freedom and peace of mind are at risk. Communicating what you want and need is tough, and dealing with the aftermath will definitely be uncomfortable and may be met with anger. Unfortunately, some relationships may be so intricately tied to long-term boundary violations that loved ones may choose to leave rather than respect your limits and independence.

As much as you may care for someone, you are not responsible for their decisions or their life. People are free to make their own decisions—including bad ones. We learn by experience and most challenges we face are just life lessons we need to learn. You are not responsible for "fixing" what others have gotten themselves into. People with healthy boundaries don't spend their time or money cleaning up other people's messes.

Boundaries define roles in relationships. They establish acceptable and unacceptable behaviors. Setting boundaries will often result in resistance and angry responses such as arguments, defensiveness, or ghosting/silent treatment—a form of passive-aggressive behavior, a punishment for daring to establish boundaries.

When people respond in an unhealthy way, it's a sign that you should have set limits a long time ago. This type of response may be an indication that they didn't really care about you, but about what you could do for them.

Boundaries protect your peace, your time, and your energy. Without them, you lose yourself in trying to please everyone else. Losing yourself is far worse than losing a few people who perhaps were never meant to stay.

> *If you want to live an authentic, meaningful life, you need to master the art of disappointing and upsetting others, hurting feelings, and living with the reality that some people just won't like you.*
> ~Cheryl Richardson,
> *The Art of Extreme Self-Care*

PROTECT YOUR BOUNDARIES

IOWA KITCHEN TABLE WISDOM

TOUGH TIMES DON'T LAST, TOUGH PEOPLE DO

When everything seems to be going against you, remember that the airplane takes off against the wind, not with it.
~Henry Ford

The title is attributed to televangelist, motivational speaker, and pastor Robert H. Schuller, founder of the Crystal Cathedral in California, best known for his TV program *Hour of Power*.

Setbacks, failures, and tragedies are all part of life. These periods of difficulty are just moments of time that will ultimately pass. How we deal with these challenges will depend on our resilience—our determination to forge through the tough moments without giving up.

Every adversity, every failure and every heartache carries with it the seed of an equivalent or a greater benefit.
            ~Napoleon Hill

Emotional resilience is the key to not just surviving but thriving. It means being able to adapt to life's misfortunes and setbacks. It helps us to adapt and cope with life's challenges with recognition that things are not always as bad as they seem.

Resilience won't make problems go away, but it will help you deal with tough situations—not giving up, not losing hope. You will still feel the anger, grief or pain, but keep going with the knowledge that this too shall pass.

Even when the world around you is changing in ways that worry you, you can take comfort that you are not alone. Building strong, healthy relationships with neighbors, loved ones and friends can give you needed support and help guide you in good and bad times. Being an active part of a community has been shown to increase resilience, happiness, and even life span.

Community is defined as a feeling of fellowship with others as a result of sharing common attitudes, interests, and goals. Sharing space, activities, and conversation with other humans provides a sense of belonging. It allows us to relate, and even grow, as we connect with others. Putting yourself out there, participating and engaging with people and events might be uncomfortable at first, but it will reap great benefits in the long run.

Whether you are a member of a book club, a political action group, your local church, or are an active volunteer at the local soup kitchen, you will find support and encouragement through a shared humanity.

In order to keep a hopeful attitude and keep going, you need to take care of yourself—tending to your physical and emotional needs. Get plenty of sleep. Learn ways to manage stress and relax. Eat well and take time to commune with nature.

This is not the end of your world; it is only a shift. Be open to the reality that your life is likely to change. Things may never be as they were before, but be grateful for all you have. Recognize that there are good things in your life even during the most difficult times.

Know that life can improve if you take action and don't just ignore your problems. Have a plan and make every day count. Do something that gives you a sense of success and purpose—a reason to get up in the morning.

Last, but not least, don't forget to count your blessings—your friends, your health, your faith. The good things in your life can bring you some measure of happiness in even the most difficult of times. Be thankful for a beautiful sunset, for the sound of the birds, the beauty of the flowers in the park, the sound of a child's laughter.

> *Today is a gift you have been granted. Make the most of it and don't take this day for granted. Appreciate little things that are too often missed. Give thanks for the smallest of miracles. Know that you are blessed just to be here—that is miracle enough.*
> ~Unknown

Tough Times Don't Last, Tough People Do

IOWA KITCHEN TABLE WISDOM

Karma Can Be a Bitch

Your believing or not believing in karma has no effect on its existence, nor on its consequences to you. Just as a refusal to believe in the ocean would not prevent you from drowning.
> ~F. Paul Wilson

Karma is the principle of cause and effect where a person's actions, words, thoughts, and intentions determine their future experiences and destiny. It also applies to the inevitable and ethical consequences that stem from those actions. The concept of karma is from ancient Indian religions like Hinduism and Buddhism, but is expressed in western religions as well.

Whatsoever a man sows, that also shall he reap.
> ~Galatians 6:7-9 (KJV)

The principle of reaping what you sow has a more modern corollary term—the law of cause and effect—sometimes referred to as the law of the universe. The law of cause and effect simply stated is: *"for every effect in your life there is a specific cause."* This is based on the premise that we live in an orderly universe governed by laws—not laws made by man, but natural laws.

This same concept is expressed in a non-secular way with the saying, *"what goes around comes around."*

One of the key themes of Karmic Law is personal responsibility for one's life. If we want positivity and peace in our lives, the best option is to plant seeds of positivity and peace, remembering the connectivity of all humanity.

> *It is your karma to fight evil. It doesn't matter if the people that evil is being committed against don't fight back. It doesn't matter if the entire world chooses to look the other way. Always remember this. You don't live with the consequences of other people's karma. You live with the consequences of your own.*
> ~Amish Tripathi
> Author

In the Christian religion the phrase *"Am I my brother's keeper?"* occurs in Genesis 4:1-9—the story of Cain and Abel. While no one is responsible for anyone else when we are unaware or unable to interfere, failure to act when someone is committing violent acts against others if we can prevent it or speak out against it, is a Karma-generating event.

> *Dangerous consequences will follow when politicians and rulers forget moral principles. Whether we believe in God or karma, ethics is the foundation of every religion.*
> ~Dalai Lama XIV

Nor should we take pleasure from someone else's troubles—even someone we think deserves it. Schadenfreude is a German term for the act of taking pleasure or joy when learning of the downfall or suffering of another.

> *How people treat you is their karma; how you react is yours.*
> ~Wayne Dyer

The effect of karma will generally not be immediately apparent. It can occur later in one's current life, and even, according to some belief systems, in future lives. If there are good things happening in your life, consider what of your past actions may have set them in motion. Likewise, with bad things. Every choice we make carries consequences that can shape our future. Some decisions have a long afterlife with an eventual outcome that is unforeseen. Even seemingly small actions can set something in motion we didn't plan on.

> *What evil is done here by man, although he thinks that he does it secretly, as it were, still it makes it manifest.*
> ~Jaiminiya Upanishad Brahmana

Life would be much easier if all our decisions were between choices that were obviously right or obviously wrong. But the reality is, which choices are right and which are wrong is often unclear.

Every choice is a cause, and every cause has an effect. Once you begin to view decisions and actions from a Karmic view, you can choose to make better choices leading to more positive outcomes.

We generally get out of life what we put in, and you generally will reap what you sow. If you work hard, you will be more successful. If you treat people the way that you want to be treated, you are more likely to be treated better by others. If you enable and facilitate darkness and despair, then you will remain in darkness and despair.

Whether you believe in the law of Karma or not, does not change reality. It's obvious from a psychological, spiritual, and practical viewpoint, the more negative thoughts and actions you engage in, the more likely you are to attract negative people into your life, and the more likely you are to have negative outcomes.

One of the hardest things to do is to look in the mirror and take full responsibility for what is happening in your life. Every action and every decision has consequences.

> *A human being fashions his consequences as surely as he fashions his goods or his dwelling. Nothing that he says, thinks or does is without consequences.*
> ~Norman Cousins
> Political journalist

IOWA KITCHEN TABLE WISDOM

LET YOUR LIFE SPEAK

What does it profit, my brethren, if someone says he has faith but does not have works? Can faith save him? If a brother or sister is naked and destitute of daily food, and one of you says to them, "Depart in peace, be warmed and filled," but you do not give them the things which are needed for the body, what does it profit? Thus also faith by itself, if it does not have works, is dead.
~James 2:14-17 (NIV)

The title comes from a Quaker saying that directs us to look at our day to day lives, and what our actions and interactions with others say about us in comparison to what we profess. Our life and our way of engaging with the world speaks to who we are and what our values and ethics are.

The quote from the epistle of James encourages

us to live in a way that is consistent with our professed beliefs, truths, and values. The choices we make and the way we treat others should be a reflection of our spiritual beliefs. When we step out into the world, every act is a testament to our beliefs and values.

> *You cannot get through a single day without having an impact on the world around you. What you do makes a difference, and you have to decide what kind of difference you want to make.*
> ~Jane Goodall
> Anthropologist

Letting your life speak is not about what you believe or how many biblical passages you can recite, or how often you attend church. It's about living with intention and integrity.

> *Integrity goes beyond speaking the truth to include taking responsibility for how one thinks and feels and what one does.*
> ~Ben Dean, Ph.D.

It's not easy to live your values. It may mean taking a position opposite that of a friend or family member—not to change minds, but to uphold your principles when you are asked to support or participate in something that violates your conscience or standards. Violating your ethics is too high a price to pay to keep the peace.

LET YOUR LIFE SPEAK

When this situation arises, it's important to be respectful and non-judgmental while remaining true and steadfast to your principles.

Letting your life speak it isn't something you do once in a while, it's something you consciously choose every day. If you are not true to yourself, how can you be true to others?

> *Integrity is doing the right thing when you don't have to—when no one else is looking or will ever know—when there will be no congratulations or recognition for having done so.*
> ~Charles Marshall

You've likely heard the expression *"practice what you preach."* In Matthew 23:3, Jesus tells the crowds and his disciples to listen to what the Pharisees and the scribes teach them, *"but do not do as they do, for they do not practice what they teach."*

Today is no different than it was in Jesus' time. The world is filled with hypocrites—people who pretend to be something they are not. They say one thing and then do the opposite. They are good at telling other people what they should do and how they should live, but fail to follow their own professed ethics and beliefs.

Letting your life speak does not mean adopting unrealistic values and standards and then working to conform your life to them. Your life cannot be based on some externally mandated view of morals with a simplistic list of good deeds, positive beliefs, and ethical standards that can be checked off a "to do" list. Trying to live by some theoretical norm will invariably fail.

As a society, we tend to look for guidance and standards from the outside world when we should listen for guidance from within. Before you can let your life speak, you must let it speak to you. Listen to your life telling you who you are. Let your conscience and instincts tell you what truths you represent, what values you hold—the standards by which you cannot help but live in order to be your authentic self.

There is no "one size fits all." You cannot dictate to the quiet, deep voice within your soul that knows your truths. The soul speaks when you are ready to listen.

You will know when you violate your own internal rules. Deep in your soul you will know, and suffer the anguish and despair of having violated your inner truth. And you will learn.

Let Your Life Speak

Iowa Kitchen Table Wisdom

PICKING AT OLD WOUNDS WON'T HEAL THEM

> *When you choose to forgive those who hurt you in the past, you take away their power over you. As long as you choose to relive the pain, you will keep those wounds from healing, poisoning your heart against those who love you today.*
> ~Unknown

Healing the psychological and emotional distress associated with past events is not easy. The more traumatic, the more difficult it is. Things that happened in the past—no matter how long ago—have a way of sticking to us and interfering with our current life and relationships.

When we can't let go of the past, it's like we make sad stories play nonstop in our heads. The more we watch, the more it hurts. We know it's not healthy, and it's interfering with our life, but no matter how hard we try, we can't seem to stop the "reruns."

It's normal to struggle with letting go of past wounds, and it can be especially difficult to disentangle yourself from actual trauma. Just because the experience is over doesn't mean the wound is healed. Holding resentment, anger, and hurt long past the event will continue to impact your ability to live a fully free life. It's like picking at a physical injury, continually reopening the wound and recreating the pain. It impairs the healing process and causes even greater injury.

Letting go can be scary, but it's an act of freedom and healing. Accepting what happened doesn't minimize or invalidate the experience you've gone through. Likewise, anger and resentment doesn't take away yesterday's trauma, but it does take away today's peace. Holding resentment is like drinking poison and expecting the other person to die.

> *Forgiveness is not always easy. At times, it feels more painful than the wound we suffered to forgive the one that inflicted it. And yet, there is no peace without forgiveness.*
> ~Marianne Williamson

PICKING AT OLD WOUNDS, WON'T HEAL THEM

Know that you are not alone. Statistics show that approximately 60% of men and 51% of women have experienced at least one traumatic event in their lifetime that led to a temporary or long-term decline in their emotional, physical, or interpersonal well-being. The most commonly reported long-term effects were trouble maintaining relationships, and increased or problematic drug or alcohol use.

The first step toward letting go of the events and wounds of the past is choosing to do so. Cutting the emotional attachment you have with the past, especially negative experiences, is not going to be easy. You will need to make peace with your past, acknowledging that although it was painful, it is always going to be a part of your past. You can't undo it. You can't make it simply go away. By continuing to let your past control your present, you are trading todays peace in order to relive yesterday's trauma.

Healing will involve a lot of emotional unpacking—and that may take some time, and possibly professional help. The longer you have held the resentments and anger, the more difficult it will be to let them go. They have become a part of who you are, how you view your world, and how you act and interact with other people. You have allowed those past events to define who you are. Letting go of the past is not forgetting what happened, it's taking back your power and saying "no more!"

You can't change what happened, but with a determined vision of a happier, freer, healthier future, healing is possible. By coming to terms with your past, and appreciating the blessings in your life now, you can change your future.

PICKING AT OLD WOUNDS, WON'T HEAL THEM

IOWA KITCHEN TABLE WISDOM

COUNT YOUR BLESSINGS

> *When you are grateful for everything that you already have and realize how blessed you are, you create space for more blessings to come into your life. The Universe loves a grateful heart. Always appreciate life and tune into abundance.*
> ~Pawan Nair
> *The Higher Self*

There is some anecdotal evidence that the idiom "Count Your Blessings" is of Jewish origin. There was an ancient Jewish tradition whereby the Rabbis taught that we should recognize and be thankful for 100 blessings each day. It was believed that this was a way of acknowledging God in all aspects of life.

Regardless of your religious leanings, this practice reminds us that no matter what is happening in our life or in the world, we have many things to be grateful for. Counting our blessings would not be a bad idea for all of us. The single most impactful thing you can do today to enrich your life is to start being grateful for what you already have.

The multitude of benefits of counting your blessings are backed by religion and science. Acknowledging and being grateful for what you have can help improve your well-being, performance, sleep, relationships, blood pressure, and stress levels.

This might sound simple but it can be difficult to put into practice. When you're facing adversities, taking the time to count your blessings may be a challenge. Even when you recognize all the positive things you should be thankful for, you can still feel terribly unhappy and possibly even guilty for feeling ungrateful.

For many people, truly feeling appreciative and grateful takes practice. The human brain is adept at identifying threats and challenges, allowing us to safely navigate through a sometimes dangerous world. But it also can skew your perception toward the negative.

So what can you do?

Make it a regular practice to count your blessings—to find good in people, places, and events. Many of the biggest blessings in life come through little moments that pass by unnoticed if you're not actively counting your blessings. By creating a regular "gratitude attitude" your brain will begin to notice and remember more of the good that happens in your life—and the more you acknowledge, the more you will see.

> *Reflect upon your present blessings of which every man has many—not on your past misfortunes, of which all men have some.*
> *~Charles Dickens*

The Bible emphasizes the importance of being grateful and counting our blessings. It teaches us to focus on the good things in our lives and to be thankful for them. Regardless of whether you are religious or not, by recognizing and appreciating your blessings, you can cultivate a positive attitude and a sense of contentment in your life. Gratitude in any form has a healing effect and can lighten the mind and make you feel happier.

Actively recognizing and appreciating the blessings in our life means knowing who we are, what matters to us, and what makes our life meaningful. When we feel grateful it puts us in a positive frame of mind, connecting us to the world and to those around us.

The benefits of gratitude are endless. Researchers have found an overwhelming connection between gratitude and good health. An attitude of gratitude alleviates stress, improves sleep quality, enhances health, brings happiness, and builds emotional awareness and stability. Focusing on what we are grateful for is a universally rewarding way to feel happier and more fulfilled. It may even lengthen our lives.

Gratitude has been one of the most widely studied activities contributing to well-being. It has been shown to have a profoundly positive impact. It supports our wellbeing with long lasting effects including boosting our mood, increasing our patience, and reducing symptoms of depression and anxiety, and even improving markers of cardiovascular health. The neuroscience of gratitude shows it activates brain regions associated with reward, enhanced feelings of contentment and emotional wellbeing.

> *Make it a habit to talk about blessings more than burdens. When you spread positivity, the Universe blesses you with even more blessings. Close the window that triggers you, no matter how captivating it is. Be disciplined about what you entertain. Where focus goes, energy flows.*
>
> ~Unknown

COUNT YOUR BLESSINGS

Part of the reason we take our blessings (including relationships) for granted is because it takes deliberate intention to stop, recognize, and appreciate what we have. By quieting the negative thoughts that turn us against ourselves and the people we love, we can feel more gratitude for the blessings of our life. It is the trigger for experiencing true joy.

> *You were given life; it is your duty (and also your entitlement as a human being) to find something beautiful within life, no matter how slight.*
> ~Elizabeth Gilbert

Iowa Kitchen Table Wisdom

LIVE SIMPLY, LOVE RICHLY

To lead a simple life. First reduce your greeds. Then reduce your needs.
~Ritu Ghatourey

The title is a command to focus on the people, freedom, joy, and flexibility of a simple life unhampered by constant demands, and focus on the things that are important rather than the stuff that isn't.

The correlation for the title is *"Live Richly, Love Poorly,"* suggesting that those who focus on making money and growing wealthy tend to prioritize the financial aspect of life and neglect the personal, leading to poor relationships.

Living simply is not a new concept. It's one of the very foundations of the Quaker religion founded in 17th century England. The Quaker simplicity testimony advocates that a person ought to live a simple life in order to focus on what is most important—that a person's spiritual life and character are more important than the quantity of goods he possesses or his monetary worth.

Nineteenth century author and philosopher Henry David Thoreau was of French-Scottish Quaker heritage. He spent more than two years living the simple life in a small house on the shore of Walden Pond near Concord, Massachusetts, where he wrote a book about his experience: *Walden, or Life in the Woods,* a testimony to the benefits of living simply. His advice to readers was "simplify, simplify."

The 1960s and early '70s ushered in a modern version of living simply as the hippie counterculture re-introduced the concept with communal living, rejection of material goods, and a Thoreau-like appreciation for nature. John Lennon urged the world to "imagine no possessions" and "nothing to kill or die for," in his song *Imagine.*

Marie Kondo, a Japanese organizing consultant, author, and TV presenter, introduced voluntary simplicity to 21st century readers in her 2014 bestseller, *The Life-Changing Magic of Tidying Up: The Japanese Art of Decluttering and Organizing,* in which she urged readers to "Keep only those things that speak to the heart, and discard items that no longer spark joy. "

> *Simplify your life. Don't waste the years struggling for things that are unimportant. Don't burden yourself with possessions. Keep your needs and wants simple and enjoy what you have. Don't destroy your peace of mind by looking back, worrying about the past. Live in the present. Simplify!*
> ~Henry David Thoreau

Today's consumer culture promises happiness and social status with expensive designer clothing, luxury cars, and larger, more extravagant homes. The never-ending pursuit of money has long been a driving factor for individuals to work harder, reach higher, and achieve more in pursuit of comfort, luxury, and security only to discover that although money can buy material possessions, it cannot fulfill the deeper needs of the human spirit.

> *Money can buy a house, but not a home; a bed, but not rest; food, but not an appetite; medicine, but not health; information, but not wisdom; thrills, but not joy; associates, but not friends; servants, but not loyalty; flattery, but not respect.*
> ~Pat Williams

There isn't a right or wrong answer for how to live simply. Everyone has a different frame of reference for what simple living means to them. Living simply is an individual choice.

The first step is about clarifying your values. It's important to recognize that your "stuff" can hold you back from the things that are most meaningful to you. That's why one of the basics of living simply is focusing on the things that are important and discarding the rest, creating more space in your life for the things and people that you love and that make you happy. Living simply is not just about living with fewer things money can buy, but about wanting less in the first place.

> *Be a curator of your life. Slowly cut things out until you're left only with what you love—with what's necessary—with what makes you happy.*
> ~Leo Babauta

There are many ways to incorporate simple living into your life. Whether you want to create a less complicated and more meaningful life or because you want to reduce the negative impact on the environment, the benefits to your health, your pocketbook, your relationships, and the environment are obvious.

LIVE SIMPLY, LOVE RICHLY

Living simply isn't just about decluttering, although that's a part of it. It's about being truly "present" in your life—slowing down, breathing deep, and finding joyful childlike wonder in everyday things. It means truly seeing a sunset, hearing the birds, smelling the fall leaves. It means awakening your senses. It means being thankful for friends, family, and the smiles of strangers. It means actively being part of the universe—not just taking up space.

> *The secret to happiness, you see, is not found in seeking more, but in developing the capacity to enjoy less.*
>
> ~Socrates

IOWA KITCHEN TABLE WISDOM

WE'RE ALL IN THIS TOGETHER

Today, if we have no peace, it is because we have forgotten that we belong to each other.
~Mother Theresa.

The title is a profound reminder of our shared humanity. Despite our differences, regardless of our race, religion, political affiliation, or nationality, we all seek the same things for ourselves, our family, and our community—prosperity, health, freedom, and equality.

From the beginning, humans have formed communities. In the dawn of time these communities were based on shared practical, basic needs—food, shelter, safety, etc. As humanity developed, the communities became more defined and divided by political, religious, and social beliefs. These beliefs developed into governance structures that further divided humanity by color, race, and tribe.

We all are part of multiple communities—our neighborhood, our city, and our state. We have a work community, a social (friends) community, a school community, and a religious community. Even our family group is a type of community.

On a larger scale, we are all part of a community that mirrors prehistoric community concepts (albeit on a much more complex level)—the community of mankind. Modern technological advances have made the entire world a community that we are part of whether we acknowledge it or not.

John Muir, naturalist, author, environmental philosopher, observed

> *When we try to pick out anything by itself, we find it hitched to everything else in the Universe.*

This is especially apropos in a world where a disaster on the other side of the planet can disrupt prices at the grocery store in a small town in Kansas, or a diseased animal in a Chinese wet market results in the death of more than a half million people in the U.S.

WE'RE ALL IN THIS TOGETHER

Realize that everything connects to everything else.
~Leonardo da Vinci

We live in a globalized world. There is a global connection between people, countries, and economies. We are part of a community where we are responsible for the other members. We are all global citizens of this big blue ball we call earth.

All of our lives have become globalized; whether through the Internet, the way in which we're impacted by the global economy, our ethical responsibility for providing humanitarian assistance to disaster victims in other countries and even in our love of world art, music, and food. As global citizens that are part of an emerging world community our actions contribute to building the global community's values and practices.

As members of this greater community, our values should reflect the moral ideals that most of us believe in—human rights, religious pluralism, participatory governance, protection of the environment, poverty reduction, sustainable economic growth, elimination of weapons of mass destruction, prevention and cessation of conflict between countries, humanitarian assistance, and the preservation and appreciation of the world's cultural diversity.

All around the world, governments and international organizations are making the policies shaping our world, from international treaties that ban the spread of nuclear weapons to administrative rules and regulations governing the internet.

Recognizing that we are members of a global community doesn't mean that we give up being a member of other communities, e.g., our town, our country, our ethnicity. It means that our more local communities need to have values that support those at the global level.

A community is based on shared values and mutual care. Being part of a community emphasizes connection, shared responsibility, service, belonging, and mutual support. The greatness of a community is measured by whether the collective actions lead to positive change, greater joy, and overall well-being for all members of the community and the larger communities in which it exists.

As part of a global community, we exist in relationship to all of humanity, knowing that our happiness and well-being is ultimately bound with the happiness and well-being of everyone else. This holds true not just ethically and spiritually, but economically and politically. As expressed in the song *None of Us Are Free* recorded by Ray Charles, *"when one of us is in chains, none of us are free."*

Being part of a community is much more than just belonging or contributing to a church, a movement, or an organization. It involves active participation. It's about doing something together that makes a difference in the lives of people we may never meet.

It takes active community participation to build vibrant, inclusive, and resilient societies able to withstand whatever comes along. Where there is a sense of belonging, there is strength. When you actively participate in your communities at every level, you not only contribute to the betterment of society at large, but also benefit personally through increased social support and improved mental well-being.

For many years now, our country and our world has felt like a powder keg ready to ignite. We are living in troubled times. There is an urgent need for respectful dialogue and understanding, and it starts with our smallest communities—our families, our churches, our schools, our local and national government—that have been torn apart, politically, weighing heavily on the collective psyche of the nation and the world.

The response cannot be to look the other way because "it doesn't affect me," or pretend there is no problem. This is an incredibly challenging time for all of us.

Current events leave us no choice but to embrace the call. We must recognize and repair our broken world—starting with electing leaders who see, understand, and support the concept that working with international groups to address the issues of global warming, global health, and peaceful resolutions to conflict is in the highest and best interests of our nation and the rest of the world.

We are truly, all in this together, and together we can move forward as a nation that stands for, and upholds, our self-evident truths and unalienable rights of life, liberty and the pursuit of happiness for all. The health and well-being of our nation and the planet depends on it.

> *We all do better when we work together. Our differences do matter, but our common humanity matters more.*
> ~Bill Bradley

We're All in This Together

Iowa Kitchen Table Wisdom

LET PEACE BEGIN WITH ME

> *Without inner peace, outer peace is impossible. We all wish for world peace, but world peace will never be achieved unless we first establish peace within our own minds. We can send so-called 'peacekeeping forces' into areas of conflict, but peace cannot be imposed from the outside with guns. Only by creating peace within our own mind and helping others to do the same can we hope to achieve peace in this world.*
> ~Geshe Kelsang Gyatso

The chapter title is from the song *Let There Be Peace On Earth* written by Jill Jackson and Sy Miller in 1955. It was initially written for and sung by the International Children's Choir. The song is performed worldwide throughout the year, but especially during the Christmas season. It's included in Sunday services of many Christian denominations.

Finding peace today is no easy task. Whether it's personal inner peace, national peace, or world peace, there seems to be no solution.

Seeing the daily realities of this planet and this country, you may be tempted to give up entirely. There's just too much hatred. Too much ignorance. Too much evil. The world as we know it is crumbling. It may feel like you are living in the wrong reality now—like there has been some kind of rupture in the space-time continuum—that the universe has gone off-balance. You may feel afraid, helpless, and full of rage.

We want to believe that most people are well-intentioned; that they care about their families and their neighbors, respect the law and the golden rule. Yet we are reminded on a daily basis of the veracity of hate in our country and around the world. History shows that hate has very deep roots, often pushing aside love and hope—and especially peace. Humans have a long evolutionary history of violence.

This brings up the question of whether there is a human predisposition toward hatred and violence. Is this the norm and not the anomaly?

Are we witnessing today, around the world and in our country, an ancient legacy of hate that is hard-wired in the brain just lying in wait to be activated?

The reality is, there have always been hateful factions in every society who prey on the vulnerable and stir up deep-seated tendencies toward hatred, cruelty, violence and war. There is hate in the world because human beings are easily indoctrinated by peer groups, social media, misplaced loyalties, and unbalanced political leaders who seek to gain power through the promotion of hate and violence.

So, how do we as individuals find peace in our mind, hearts, and in our lives? It starts with the thoughts we think, the words we speak, and the actions we take. True peace doesn't come in a pill or a bottle.

> *World peace must develop from inner peace. Peace is not just mere absence of violence. Peace is, I think, the manifestation of human compassion.*
> *~Dalai Lama XIV*

The scripture says in Colossians 3:15 (AMPC) to let peace act as an umpire. This is saying that peace should be the deciding factor when it comes to our responses to those who think, look, act, believe, or worship differently from us.

In today's world, we find chaos, discontent, divisions, and hate. Where is peace? Peace comes when there is love to give it birth, nurture it along, and cause it to endure. Peace is love in action.

We are very good at finding reasons to not be at peace. Lord knows, we don't need to look very hard these days. Just turn on the news for 15 minutes and you can forget peaceful feelings for the rest of the day!

Peace does not depend on external factors, it begins within our own mind! If we are convinced that we will never find inner peace, then we will be right.

> *Ego says, "Once everything falls into place, I'll feel peace." Spirit says "find your peace and everything will fall into place."*
> ~Marianne Williamson

True inner peace can never be achieved so long as we are focused on past events or future worries. The past is gone and can never be changed. It isn't real and only exists in our memory; and memories can be flawed—influenced by our emotions and interpretations. Letting go of what no longer serves creates space for a mindful approach to life. We can never find inner peace while nurturing resentment about past perceived offenses.

> *When something you have absolutely no control over is making you unhappy, stop giving it free rent in the mind.*
> ~Ancient Buddhist saying

The future hasn't yet happened, and only exists in our imagination. The mind can only guess at what the future will look like.

It's only right now, today—one minute at a time—that is real. Focusing on the past and future disconnects you from where you are now. The ground on which your new life will grow and blossom is right here—right now. You can't rewind the world to the way things were before or control how things will be in the future. Be mindful of the present—it's the only time that matters.

> *The past is gone, the future is not here, now I am free of both. Right now, I choose joy.*
> ~Deepak Chopra

Acknowledge the reality of what is happening, but don't give up. Sometimes the worst place you can live is in your own head. You may not be able to control what is happening around you, but you can control how you respond to it.

> *We but mirror the world. All the tendencies present in the outer world are to be found in the world of our body. If we could change ourselves, the tendencies in the world would also change. As a man changes his own nature, so does the attitude of the world change towards him. This is the divine mystery supreme. A wonderful thing it is and the source of our happiness. We need not wait to see what others do.*
> ~Mahatma Gandhi

An old saying goes: *"In order to grow flowers, you need to disturb the soil."* Although the world is broken, consider that perhaps the Universe is tilling the soil for a better, kinder world to emerge.

> *Do not be dismayed by the brokenness of the world. All things break. And all things can be mended. Not with time, as they say, but with intentions.*
> *So go. Love intentionally, extravagantly, unconditionally. The broken world waits in darkness for the light that is you.*
> ~L. R. Knost

LET PEACE BEGIN WITH ME

Iowa Kitchen Table Wisdom

FORGIVENESS IS FOR THE FORGIVER

We must develop and maintain the capacity to forgive. He who is devoid of the power to forgive is devoid of the power to love. Forgiveness is not an occasional act, it is a constant attitude.
~Dr. Martin Luther King, Jr.

Forgiving isn't something you do for someone else. It's something you do for yourself. Often the person we are forgiving will never know they have been forgiven, but we have made a decision to no longer be tied to that individual by resentment and anger. We forgive to free ourselves.

Forgiving is a movement of your heart not to carry aversive hatred or blame. That you can care about someone and still create boundaries.
~Tara Brach

Forgiveness isn't easy. We resist letting go of the

hurt when someone has harmed us—especially when we believe it was deliberate.

> *When we have been betrayed and wounded, when we are threatened and afraid, holding onto resentment is a way of protecting ourselves. It is our way of armoring against the experience of raw pain.*
> ~Tara Brach

Forgiveness does not mean you're okay with what happened, nor does it mean that you will feel good, nor does it ignore the harm or trauma of the wrongdoing. It is merely an acceptance—coming to terms with the reality that it happened and can't be undone.

If we wait for the other person to apologize, we often will end up bearing that burden our whole lives. In that case, we are the ones who suffer.

> "Not forgiving is like drinking rat poison and then waiting for the rat to die."
> ~Anne Lamott

Forgiveness doesn't involve forgetting or ignoring. Unfortunately some people hold grudges, unable to let go of the anger towards those who they believe "wronged" them. Breakups, family trauma, or betrayal can easily cause resentment and subsequent grudges to take root. The problem with grudges is they don't change anything—they don't heal our hurt and they don't make us feel any better.

Holding a grudge often ends up causing emotional, physical, and social issues, so it's important to learn to cope in a healthier way. Grudges may also result in persistent re-runs in your head about the person and/or incident. This is particularly common when you think someone has done something intentionally or you have no idea what you did to warrant their behavior—especially if they don't seem to care. Holding a grudge will inhibit your ability to cope with or resolve your issue and keep you trapped in the unpleasant event or interaction.

There is a saying *"Hurt people, hurt people,"* meaning that those who have been hurt, often inflict pain on others. Their original hurt is like a wound that an innocent statement, oversight, or action can tear open, causing misunderstanding and unwarranted lashing out at others. Unfortunately, people who have had pain or trauma in their own lives are inclined to inflict abuse on others, creating a never-ending cycle.

We all have emotional injuries. The longer we harbor them, the longer they will burden us. Forgiveness doesn't involve forgetting or ignoring what has happened. Forgiving more, leads to loving more.

> *Forgiveness is a sign that the person who has wronged you means more to you than the wrong they have dealt.*
> ~Ben Greenhalgh

There is no end to forgiveness. Forgiveness is a lifelong process. We will continue to go through life being reminded and triggered by old trauma, slights, or abuse, and that old pain will once again take hold of us. Each time it happens provides another opportunity to practice compassion and courage as we again forgive and remain open to love.

> *Then Peter came to Him and said, "Lord, how often shall my brother sin against me, and I forgive him? Up to seven times?" Jesus said to him, "I do not say to you, up to seven times, but up to seventy times seven."*
> ~Matthew 18:21-22 (NKJV)

Forgiveness is For the Forgiver

Love Your Neighbor As Yourself

> *For you, brothers, were called to freedom; but do not use your freedom as an opportunity for the flesh. Rather, serve one another in love. The entire law is fulfilled in a single decree: "Love your neighbor as yourself." But if you keep on biting and devouring one another, watch out, or you will be consumed by one another.*
> ~Galatians 5:13-15 (BSB)

The title and the quotation are a message with a warning that if we do not take care of each other, we will all suffer.

Our faith and our ethics are being tested. We are first-hand witnesses to great cruelty that is systemic and part of the failure of the larger political system. Systems that were designed to protect us from our "lesser instincts" are breaking into little pieces strewn along the highway of democracy.

We are going through not just a political crisis, but a spiritual one—but not the one Christian Nationalists are railing about. The spiritual soul of the country has been misappropriated by purveyors of hate and division intent on re-interpreting the gospel for their own benefit—turning neighbor against neighbor, and elevating the cruel and greedy in the name of religion.

The message of "love your neighbor" has become an urgent call to action as the powers-that-be are so out of step with it. The American myth of self-sufficiency has become a justification for selfishness. America is in a time of testing like no other in the 250 years of existence—and so far, we're failing miserably!

Even though "love your neighbor as yourself" is a simple statement, it is the basis of Christian theology, and is fundamental for most other religions as well. The hostility and cruelty perpetrated, and even legislated, by people who claim to be acting in the name of Judeo-Christian values, is the very antithesis of nearly ALL religious teachings.

LOVE YOUR NEIGHBOR AS YOURSELF

A religion that is so disconnected from humanity and whose sole purpose serves the individual's personal benefit, without regard for others and the collective well-being, is just dogma. That type of religion does a lot more than just separate us as a society. It fractures and pits us against each other as a world.

> *You in the West have the spiritually poorest of the poor. I find it easy to give a plate of rice to a hungry person, but to console or to remove the bitterness, anger, and loneliness that comes from being spiritually deprived, that takes a long time.*
> ~Mother Teresa

When we look away from the suffering and the environmental disaster we're creating, when we judge people who are homeless or struggling, we are not acting in a spiritual way. All the great world religions encourage us to love one another—to care about the well-being of our fellow humans and the natural world. True spirituality is recognizing our sacred interconnectedness with the rest of the world and with our natural environment.

> *Learn to do right; seek justice. Defend the oppressed. Take up the cause of the fatherless; plead the case of the widow.*
> ~Isaiah 1:17 (NIV)

If we were to focus our money and energy toward creating social infrastructures to meet the basic physical and emotional needs of those who are suffering, we could maybe lower the temperature of anger, hate, and violence infecting our communities and our world. This type of social contract would help build a society geared toward reducing the fears and needs that cause or exacerbate a variety of social ills.

The reality is that a social policy rooted in humane care for our fellow humans is embedded in longstanding spiritual tradition.

> *Beware of false prophets, which come to you in sheep's clothing, but inwardly they are ravening wolves. Ye shall know them by their fruits. Do men gather grapes of thorns, or figs of thistles? Even so every good tree bringeth forth good fruit; but a corrupt tree bringeth forth evil fruit. A good tree cannot bring forth evil fruit, neither can a corrupt tree bring forth good fruit. Every tree that bringeth not forth good fruit is hewn down, and cast into the fire. Wherefore by their fruits ye shall know them.*
> ~Matthew 7:15-20 (KJV)

Bearing good fruit means loving our neighbors—ALL our neighbors—no exceptions!

LOVE YOUR NEIGHBOR AS YOURSELF

Iowa Kitchen Table Wisdom

TO HAVE A FRIEND BE ONE

Many people will walk in and out of your life, but only true friends will leave footprints in your heart
~Eleanor Roosevelt

The title quote is a variation of the quote by Ralph Waldo Emerson *"The only way to have a friend is to be one."*

We make many acquaintances in our lifetime. A few will become friends. Some will become close friends. A very special few will become lifelong friends. Those are the ones who are there for you through good times and bad, overlooking your faults and supporting your dreams.

Friends are vital for a happy and healthy life. Research shows that close friendships are associated with greater happiness, self-esteem, and sense of purpose, affecting our psychological health as well as our physical health. Spending time with friends releases endorphins in the brain and makes us happy.

Friendship is a relationship requiring mutual respect. If someone gets what they need from you and then walks away—often without explanation or warning—be glad they are out of your life. Move on with your life and count it as a lesson learned. Some people go through friends like used tissue. They may make friends easily, but when the friend fails to live up to their unrealistic expectations the friendship is over.

If a friendship is strong, you don't always have to agree on things. Occasionally, a friend may do or say something you don't agree with or find offensive. If it's a true friendship, when you disagree you will hopefully feel safe enough to talk it through. Often, the individual is unaware that they have crossed a boundary. Everyone has boundaries and deal-breakers, but preserving a friendship worth keeping may require overlooking minor slights. Genuine friendships will flourish only when mutual respect and good communication exists. Friendships require maintenance.

Friendships are unique relationships. We are drawn toward people who we see as similar to ourselves, who make us feel good, share our beliefs, and enjoy what we enjoy. In order to maintain relationships we need to know and respect each other's needs, limits, and commitments to other people in their life.

*Family loves you because they have to.
Friends love you because they choose to.*
                              ~Unknown

Levels of commitment will vary over a lifetime. How long and how close a friendship is depends on proximity and life events. As these things change, commitment may lessen.

Sometimes friendships end because of changes in our life or our friend's life. We move away, start a new job, get busy with family responsibilities, retire, or interests change. Sometimes our priorities just no longer align. So how do we maintain friendships that we cherish when life interferes?

It's important to keep in touch. This is much easier today than it was in the past. It doesn't take much effort to text or call people you care about. Although letter writing has gone out of style, taking the time to write a letter can go a long way toward continuing a meaningful long distance relationship. And don't forget actual birthday and holiday cards. If you are still in geographic proximity, make it a practice to meet for lunch, dinner or even coffee on a regular basis—just to "check in."

Most important of all is to be there if your friend needs your help, comfort, advice or just needs someone to listen. When we have good friends, we know we are not alone. When crisis strikes, true friends can be counted on for support.

There is an old proverb that translates from the 3rd century Latin as *"A friend in need, is a friend in deed."* This is a truism meaning your true friends will be there when you need them. Having friendships and a social network not only helps us to age better, but has been shown to have a positive effect on our overall health and longevity.

> *A friend is someone who understands your past, believes in your future, and accepts you just the way you are.*
> ~Unknown

TO HAVE A FRIEND, BE ONE

Iowa Kitchen Table Wisdom

BE MINDFUL IN WHAT YOU DO AND SAY

> *When we are mindful, deeply in touch with the present moment, our understanding of what is going on deepens, and we begin to be filled with acceptance, joy, peace and love.*
> ~Thich Nhat Hanh
> Buddhist Master

You may have been admonished as a child to "Mind your manners!" or "Mind what you say!" or "Mind where you're walking." Apparently you were doing or saying something "mindlessly" without thinking.

We may have been taught as children to *"think before you speak"* or to *"not act rashly."* Unfortunately, most Americans have historically been seen (and rightly so) by other countries as being impulsive, rash, or reckless—mindlessly speaking, acting, and reacting based on emotions, without thinking, and having a total lack of concern for the consequences. These traits are the polar opposite of mindfulness!

The idea of "mindfulness" comes from Buddhist teachings and meditation. Thích Nhất Hạnh, a Vietnamese Thiền Buddhist monk, is historically recognized as the father of mindfulness. Nhất Hạnh was a major influence on Western practices of Buddhism. Buddhist enlightenment involves attention, awareness, and being present in the moment as the first step toward enlightenment.

Mindfulness has become a mainstream practice and a pivotal therapeutic technique in science and medicine in America in recent years.

Mindfulness practice has been shown to be beneficial to our physical and mental health—reducing stress, improving communications and relationships, and being more aware of how we interact with our environment and our relationships. It can bring greater inner peace and may also be used in mindfulness-based therapies to treat stress, anxiety, or pain, or simply to achieve greater relaxation.

BE MINDFUL IN WHAT YOU DO AND SAY

You've probably heard the term, but what does it mean to be mindful? Paying attention and truly being "present" with those you love is a way of connecting with your life. This is one aspect of mindfulness.

> *The way you speak to others can offer them joy, happiness, self-confidence, hope, trust, and enlightenment. Mindful speaking is a deep practice.*
> —Thich Nhat Hanh

Mindfulness means being attentive to, and aware of, our language, thoughts, feelings, bodily sensations, and the surrounding environment—being "present" in the moment without judgement. It's the practice of observing our thoughts and feelings without judging them as good or bad. It's a way of reawakening to the present, rather than dwelling on the past or focusing on the future. Mindfulness can be practiced through specific meditation sessions or in random moments throughout the day.

New research suggests that immersing oneself in nature while using mindfulness techniques, clears the mind and relaxes the senses.

Mindfulness enables us to stay more connected to the people around us and awaken to what we've been missing or taking for granted. Practicing mindfulness is an organic and effective way to tap into feelings of gratitude. When we are grateful we call more positive things into our lives.

There is a practice known as Emotional Freedom Technique (EFT) that combines tapping on acupressure points with mindful attention to release emotional blockages and reduce stress. EFT can be used alongside mindfulness-based therapies to enhance self-awareness within relationships.

The emotional and physical benefits of mindfulness include lowering stress levels, reducing harmful thoughts, and protecting against depression and anxiety. It can be helpful in understanding and coping with uncomfortable emotions, and painful memories of past events. Mindfulness practice can create happier and more satisfying relationships, cultivating empathy and compassion toward others.

> *Letting go gives us freedom, and freedom is the only condition for happiness. If, in our heart, we still cling to anything— anger, anxiety, or possessions—we cannot be free.*
> ~Thich Nhat Hanh
> Vietnamese Buddhist monk

BE MINDFUL IN WHAT YOU DO AND SAY

Iowa Kitchen Table Wisdom

LIVE AND LET LIVE

Tolerance implies no lack of commitment to one's own beliefs. Rather it condemns the oppression or persecution of others.
~John F. Kennedy

The title "Live and Let Live" is of Dutch origin, and was first recorded in 1622 in *The Ancient Law Merchant*, a system of law developed by medieval merchants to regulate commerce throughout the known world of Europe, North Africa, and Asia Minor. Much of today's commercial law is still based on the basic premises laid down by the Law Merchants.

Children today are born into and grow up in an increasingly diverse world. They are exposed early on to different beliefs, languages, foods, lifestyles, etc. In America, we are a "melting pot" of diversity—like it or not. That is actually one of our strengths! In order to successfully navigate in such a pluralistic society, we need to learn, and practice, understanding and tolerance.

Throughout history there have been wars fought, people killed or jailed, and individuals "cast out" because of intolerance. It's essential that we recognize and care for the marginalized in society.

> *Is not this the kind of fasting I have chosen: to loosen the chains of injustice and untie the cords of the yoke, to set the oppressed free and break every yoke? Is it not to share your food with the hungry and to provide the poor wanderer with shelter—when you see the naked, to clothe them, and not to turn away from your own flesh and blood?*
> ~Isaiah 58:6-7 (NIV)

Unfortunately, we are living at a time in America when tolerance for any type of diversity is disparaged and labeled "woke" and often even criminalized. When upholding the freedoms written into the Bill of Rights and the Constitution of the United States are discouraged our country is in serious spiritual trouble.

There is a large portion of American society that refuses to recognize that the success of a society and a country in what is a global environment depends on allowing others the freedom to live their lives without fear or censure.

LIVE AND LET LIVE

Many religions, schools and educators around the world had begun making tolerance part of the curriculum. That is, until any mention of tolerance, acceptance, and understanding of other races, beliefs, practices, lifestyles, etc. was relabeled "CRT," and subsequently demonized as indoctrination and brainwashing.

Intolerance often comes from those who have a narrow view of the world. These are generally individuals who are unwilling to consider alternative views, often resorting to physical violence when ideas are presented that challenge what they believe. They fear those who are different, hold different beliefs, and live different lifestyles.

> *Human beings are more alike than we are unalike. And the minute we began to understand, just the slightest part of that, we recognize ourselves as family.*
> *~Maya Angelou.*

America has become an intolerant country—one that is unwilling to accept and respect the beliefs, behavior, religious practices, and opinions of anyone who is of a different color, language, or heritage from what they have determined to be "true American." We have lost the ability to empathize with the struggles of someone who is not "like us" because it doesn't align with our own life experience.

Intolerance is not just an individual failing, it is an American societal crisis! We have lost our sense of who we are and how and why this country was founded. We have become an angry, hateful, violent people, and the blatant—even legalized—discrimination and hate has been promoted, encouraged, endorsed, and promulgated by leaders starting at the very top of our government.

Tolerance is the acceptance of ideas and lifestyles with which we may not agree and that may be incompatible with our ideas and lifestyle. It is living in such a way that we respect, and don't interfere with, the rights of others to believe and live as they choose—even if it involves something we personally wouldn't choose. As long as the belief or behavior is legal, it is none of our business.

> *I don't think we should try to convert people from one religion to another, because in spite of our different labels, we all worship the same God.*
> ~Billy Graham

It is incumbent on each of us to confront intolerance in whatever form it comes and wherever we see it. We need to practice seeing the humanity in every human being. When we treat each other with love, kindness, grace, and compassion we are acknowledging that all are members of the human race. Through this perspective, we can better experience the unity that comes from being a world community. It is only in this way that we can hope to build a more tolerant and inclusive society.

> *There is only one 'race'—the human race—*
> *and we are all members of it.*
> ~Margaret Atwood

The quote by Atwood reminds us that regardless of differences in beliefs, skin color, nationality or language, we are all human beings. It is a reminder of our unity, in spite of societal constructs that promote division and prejudice.

When we examine major religions, we find similar stories about a savior and teachings about good and evil. The Golden Rule is also common to many religions.

Hate and discrimination have been around since the beginning of humanity. In Shakespeare's *The Merchant of Venice*, Shylock asserts the equality between Christians and Jews and all other races of humans on earth. *"If you prick us, do we not bleed?"* It's a call for empathy, understanding, and solidarity among all people.

The collective strength and progress of the human race is reliant on the recognition of our shared identity and interconnectedness. We are all mortals who go through a cycle of life. We all bleed the same, and love the same, and grieve the same. We all age and die. We all have the ability to awaken to our higher selves—our better selves.

This is a call to look into your heart, to view humanity through a broader lens, one that doesn't distinguish or discriminate based on racial, religious, or ethnic lines.

If we are to survive, we need to recognize our shared humanity, our common evolutionary heritage, and our united destiny.

LIVE AND LET LIVE

Iowa Kitchen Table Wisdom

Stand Up For Your Principles

Now we have come to a time of special stress and test. There never was a time when we needed more clearly to conserve the principles of our own patriotism than this present time.
~Woodrow Wilson
DAR address, 1915

The title is a take on a modern proverb that was part of a Methodist sermon published in a 1926 Iowa newspaper.

This next year, 2026, we will be celebrating the 250th anniversary of the founding of this country. It seems strangely serendipitous that it's also a period when our democracy is being threatened— that the fundamental rights and liberties established by the founding fathers are in danger of being demolished and thrown onto the trash heap of history.

There is a growing divide in the country. The driving factor for the rising division is fear. Fear of the inevitable changes facing our nation: global warming, population decline, demographic changes, and a global decline in democracies around the world.

The nation's "diversity explosion" represents an important part of our future, a phenomenon that our policies and politics need to recognize and embrace. If not, we are heading for a demographic cliff as the population shrinks. Without immigrants to fill the gaps, we will be faced with severe skill shortages and economic challenges predicted to become critical as early as 2028 unless current anti-immigrant policies and actions change.

In addition, the world is now warming faster than at any point in recorded history. Polar ice shields are melting and the sea is rising, threatening the very future of humanity as we know it!

Last, but not least, we have seen a rise in authoritarian governments over the past two decades that is global and pervasive. More than a third of the world population now lives under authoritarian rule—and America is at risk of joining them.

STAND UP FOR YOUR PRINCIPLES

We are seeing an erosion of democracy that mirrors the path other countries took on the road to autocracy. Even though we may have expected some of this, it is way worse than anything we could have imagined.

The cold, hard truth is that we are in imminent danger of losing our democracy altogether. With his return to the presidency in 2025, Trump has taken a series of dangerous and illegal actions reminiscent of 1930's Nazi Germany: exacting retribution against political opponents; deploying armed and masked troops into American cities who randomly beat and teargas men, women, and children; threatening judges, universities, news outlets, and even state governments to do his bidding—all in blatant violation of the Constitution and multiple civil and federal laws. While this is happening Congressional Republicans sit idly by, saying and doing nothing out of fear.

> *Fear is the universal tool of authoritarians, and it is a clear sign that our democracy is in danger that so many Americans now have reason to fear their government.*
> ~New York Times

If we are to survive as a democracy, the answer apparently lies with "we the people." This country was founded on dissent, and if the people find it necessary to declare a complete rejection of the party in power whether through the election process or through forcible overthrow of the government, there is no doubt it will happen. The recent "No Kings" rally with a final count of more than 8.5 million participants in 2700+ American cities is a warning that the tide is turning. The people have had enough!

> *Power concedes nothing without a demand. It never did and it never will. Find out just what any people will quietly submit to and you have found out the exact measure of injustice and wrong which will be imposed upon them, and these will continue till they are resisted with either words or blows, or with both. The limits of tyrants are prescribed by the endurance of those whom they oppress.*
> ~Frederick Douglass

So what can we do?

The methodology of an authoritarian takeover is to commit so many outrageous and frightening actions that the citizenry will be paralyzed and confused—not knowing what things to address next. You can't fight everything, but you can fight something, in some way. Remember, dissent is the highest form of patriotism.

STAND UP FOR YOUR PRINCIPLES

The point is not to find the "perfect" thing to do, but to find something that speaks to your strengths, abilities, and interests. Get involved in whatever way makes the most sense for you. You may need to try several things before you find a good fit.

For many people, their first involvement in politics and activism isn't through a particular organization or group. Whether it's making a banner or a sign for a protest, calling your political representatives, opening your home for planning meetings, or just showing up at a protest—you can contribute.

Maybe you will find your calling by helping those who are negatively affected by the policies and actions of this regime. You can volunteer or donate to food banks, homeless shelters, Veterans centers, Habitat for Humanity, Friends of the Library, hospitals/nursing homes, Meals on Wheels, etc. The opportunity is endless.

The resistance consists of people of all ages, backgrounds, races, and religions. We all can play a part, however small. Each of us must figure out what is ours to do. You don't have to be the whole orchestra—you can just be a single note. You don't have to be the quarterback—each member of a team is critical to success. No matter your age or your physical limitations, you can participate in the act of patriotism. Join the resistance in whatever way speaks to you.

Most of all—VOTE—and work to get more voters to the polls! Voter turnout in the US is around 60% in presidential elections and 40% in midterm elections. The voter turnout in the 2024 election was 65.3%. **Statistics show that 80% turnout can totally flip the political direction of a state or a country!**

History will judge us by what we did when our country's future, our democracy, and our Constitution was under attack. Let's make America a better, stronger union—the rebirth of what our founders envisioned—by restoring and protecting what our forefathers gave birth to 250 years ago.

> *Our Constitution is a remarkable, beautiful gift. But it's really just a piece of parchment. It has no power on its own. We, the people, give it power. We, the people, give it meaning—with our participation, and with the choices that we make and the alliances that we forge.*
> *~Barack Obama*

STAND UP FOR YOUR PRINCIPLES

NEVER LOSE HOPE

The best way to not feel hopeless is to get up and do something. Don't wait for good things to happen to you. If you go out and make some good things happen, you will fill the world with hope, you will fill yourself with hope.

~Barack Obama

We are living in a time when the headlines are heavy, dark, and discouraging—with a political swing to the far right fueling violence, unemployment, economic chaos, rampant corruption, and seemingly unending cruelty to our fellow humans on a level not seen since 1930s Germany. The grief is unavoidable. It's everywhere we look, everything we hear. We see a world that is broken, with leaders who seemingly have no moral compass, no soul, no sense of humanity or compassion.

There are days when it seems that the efforts, the struggles, and the sacrifices of so many people fighting for social and environmental justice, fighting prejudice, racism and greed, are fighting a losing battle.

We're totally burned out from toxic politics and relentless global conflict. We're worried that the world as we know it might not exist for our children and grandchildren.

In a world facing political polarization, multiple wars around the world, the prospect of a warming planet, armed military occupation of our major cities, private citizens being snatched up off the street and "disappeared," it's easy to despair. Today, fear, more than hope, is characteristic of our time, and our fears are legitimate.

All of the freedoms mentioned in the First Amendment of the Constitution are under attack: freedom of religion, freedom of speech; freedom of the press; freedom of assembly; and freedom to petition the Government when it violates the Constitution or the rights outlined in the Constitution.

> *Congress shall make no law respecting an establishment of religion, or prohibiting the free exercise thereof; or abridging the freedom of speech, or of the press; or the right of the people peaceably to assemble,*

and to petition the Government for a redress of grievances."
  ~U.S. Constitution, First Amendment

In addition, we are under threat of losing our right to move about the country without "checkpoints," our right to make our own health decisions and control our own body, and the right to marry the person of our choice. This is not America as the Founding Fathers envisioned. It is the very antithesis of what they fought for.

Without good governance and honest leadership, we cannot solve our enormous social and environmental challenges.

It's true that history takes two steps forward and one step back. Even fascism is once again gaining traction—the neo-Nazis are getting stronger in America and even in Germany—who should have learned their lesson from the past! It takes time for humanity to evolve morally. Unfortunately, we don't have the luxury of time on our side.

> *History doesn't move in a straight line. History zigs and zags.*
>   ~President Barack Obama

We certainly hope it is not too late to turn things around—but sometimes hope seems impossible, and fear feels overwhelming. How can we continue to have hope for the future in the face of such a dystopian nightmare? When everything you thought you could depend on seems threatened it can be difficult to stay grounded, inspired, and open to better possibilities. Hope can seem elusive—a fool's errand, but don't confuse hope with blind optimism or wishful thinking. Hope is a personal decision to believe, often against all odds, that something better is possible. It's hope that fuels human action. True resilience comes from cultivating hope within yourself.

> *Most of the important things in the world have been accomplished by people who have kept on trying when there seemed to be no hope at all.*
> ~Dale Carnegie

There will undoubtedly be many moments of disappointment and despair ahead. No one can know how it will all turn out. The future is unknown, but embracing uncertainty means embracing possibilities. Hope is acknowledging reality while still believing in the possibility of something better. Even when facing seemingly impossible situations, hope helps you to stay present, and navigate your way through to the other side. Hopeful people won't let the darkness win. They are the rebels of the world—living to fight another day!

> *Courage doesn't always roar, sometimes it's the quiet voice at the end of the day whispering "I will try again tomorrow"*
> ~Mary Anne Radmacher

Feeling anxious and sometimes deeply depressed because of what is happening, can cause feelings of helplessness, depression, fear, fatalism, resignation, sadness, and anger. Hope is a fickle thing. You have it, and then you don't. You think everything is going back to normal, and then you hear crushing or frightening news, and hope disappears.

When the world falls apart hope becomes a survival tool. It can be tempting to throw in the towel believing that maybe this battle is not winnable. When you feel like you're on the verge of giving up, often walking away is exactly what you need to do in order to gain perspective and develop a new strategy. Defeat doesn't have to be permanent.

Sometimes the secret of success is just hanging in there and starting again tomorrow! Throughout history, when it looked as though the end was near, hope has fueled movements—systems were changed, justice was restored, the world became sane again and began to rebuild itself—stronger and better. Hope has always been the ember at the center of revolutions. To hope in a broken world is an act of resistance. To rise again to rebuild the world as it crumbles around us is the work of warriors—the ones who hope.

> *Sunflowers always turn in the direction of light because they instinctively know it's a source of strength and renewal. Take a lesson from the sunflower. Look for the light in your world.*
> ~Unknown

We cultivate hope when we stay connected to others who see what we see, who celebrate the small victories, who imagine a better future, and who take action—however small or messy—toward that better future. Hope is courage, and courage, like hope, is contagious. Healing lies in the ways we come together in community to support each other. Each of us has a role to play, no matter how small.

At a time when all looks hopeless amid a world that seems to be lost, we need hope more than ever. It is one of the great motivators for positive action during desperate times. Hope is a sign of courage and strength, an expectation of things we cannot fully control. Sometimes hope is just lurking beneath the surface, and you don't notice it's there quietly waiting to burst into awareness.

> *We must accept finite disappointment, but never lose infinite hope.*
> ~Dr. Martin Luther King, Jr.

Even against all reasonable expectations, hope helps us to go on and not give ourselves over to darkness and despair. We have to believe that humanity's willingness to cooperate for the common good will ultimately prove to be more potent than forces pulling in the other direction.

> *You may not always have a comfortable life and you will not always be able to solve all of the world's problems at once but don't ever underestimate the importance you can have, because history has shown us that courage can be contagious and hope can take on a life of its own.*
> ~Michelle Obama

We cannot sit this one out. Our freedoms are only as strong as our willingness to defend them. Whether you're left, right, or somewhere in between, the principle is the same: DEMOCRACY AND FREEDOM ARE NON-NEGOTIABLE.

Our future happiness lies not in a hope that insists on everyone behaving and believing alike, but in everyone being able to live and believe as they choose. When we are in such profound turmoil, we all need to light our internal candles of hope. When we listen to that still, small voice within, we will take the right action—we will know what is ours to do, and hope will return.

> *Hope is being able to see that there is light despite all the darkness.*
> ~Desmond Tutu

One of the most important aspects of maintaining an attitude of hope is a belief in a better future, even in the face of adversity. It's that optimistic quality that makes us tackle what seems impossible and never give up, despite the odds, despite the scorn or mocking, despite possible failure. With courage and determination the impossible becomes possible. The difficult is hard, the impossible just takes a little longer.

On 6 June 1966 in Capetown, South Africa, Robert F. Kennedy gave a speech called *Day of Affirmation* in which he encouraged hope:

> *First is the danger of futility; the belief there is nothing one man or one woman can do against the enormous array of the world's ills—against misery, against ignorance, or injustice and violence. Yet many of the world's great movements, of*

> *thought and action, have flowed from the work of a single man.*
>
> *...Few will have the greatness to bend history; but each of us can work to change a small portion of the events, and in the total of all these acts will be written the history of this generation.*
>
> *...Each time a man stands up for an ideal, or acts to improve the lot of others, or strikes out against injustice, he sends forth a tiny ripple of hope, and crossing each other from a million different centers of energy and daring those ripples build a current which can sweep down the mightiest walls of oppression and resistance.*

There is hope for our future—for the health of our planet, our societies, and our children, but only if we all work together and join forces. Hope is a social gift we share with each other.

The future is not something we wait for. It is something we build—with our hearts, our words, our actions, and our votes. Hope is not about guarantees. The people who succeed are those who won't give up, who, when one battle is lost, gear up for the next. It's about recognizing that we may be planting seeds in a garden we will never see bloom.

IOWA KITCHEN TABLE WISDOM

SUGGESTED READING

Browne, Harry. *How I Found Freedom in an Unfree World*. Independently published, 2014.

Carnegie, Dale. *How to Stop Worrying and Start Living: Time-Tested Methods for Conquering Worry*. V&S Publishers, re-issued 2022.

Cole-Whittaker, Terry. *What You Think of Me is None of My Business*. Berkley Publishing, 1988.

Earle, David W. *Love is Not Enough: Changing Dysfunctional Family Habits*. 2014.

Foster, Jeff. *The Way of Rest: Finding The Courage to Hold Everything in Love*. Sounds True Publishing, 2016.

Foster, Jeff. *The Deepest Acceptance: Radical Awakening in Ordinary Life*. Sounds True Publishing, 2012.

Goodall, Jane and Douglas Abrams. *The Book of Hope: A Survival Guide for Trying Times.* Celadon Books, 2021.

Gulley, Philip. *Living the Quaker Way: Discover the Hidden Happiness in the Simple Life.* Convergent Books, 2014.

Hart, Gary. *The American Republic Can Save American Democracy.* Fulcrum Publishing, 2022.

Hersey, Paul. *The Situational Leader.* Center for Leadership Studies, 1986.

Hill, Napoleon. *Outwitting the Devil: The Secrets to Freedom and Success.* Sound Wisdom Publishing, 2020.

Walsch, Neale Donald. *The New Revelations: A Conversation with God.* Atria Publishing, 2002.

Williamson, Marianne. *The Gift of Change: Spiritual Guidance for a Radically New Life.* Harper Publishing, 2004.

Ziglar, Zig and Julie Ziglar Norman. *Embrace the Struggle: Living Life on Life's Terms.* Howard Books, 2009/2013.

Suggested Reading

J. L. Wertis Books

The Longest Four Years: *The Trump Administration's Assault on Democracy, and the Rise of White Nationalism*

Alternate Reality: *The Ultimate Guide to the Mad, Mad World of Conspiracy Theories*

Lies, Crimes and Other Political Skullduggery: *The Informed Voters Guide to Political Terms, Concepts, and Claims Heard on the News*

Project 2025: *An Authoritarian Takeover of the United States*

Making Good Trouble: *A Political Action Handbook*

We're All Just Walking Each Other Home: *Messages of Hope, Love, and Peace for a Troubled World*

It's the Economy, Stupid!: *The Coming Economic Crisis*

Available on *Amazon.com*

Iowa Kitchen Table Wisdom

ABOUT THE AUTHOR

J. L. Wertis is a non-fiction author who writes in the genres of sociology, self-help, philosophy, politics, and family history.

Ms. Wertis did her undergraduate studies in Psychology/Sociology at the University of Nebraska at Omaha. She has a Bachelor of Science in Computer Information Systems, a Master's in Business Administration/Law, and did post graduate work in Social Sciences and Psychology—a dissertation short of a PhD.

Throughout the years she has maintained an active interest in studying how social and political influences, perceptions and interactions affect individual and group behavior. This interest adds depth to her political and historical works.

She is a member of PEN America, a 100 year old nonprofit that defends the right to expression through the written word, protecting the right to write, read and learn.

www.ingramcontent.com/pod-product-compliance
Lightning Source LLC
Chambersburg PA
CBHW061638040426
42446CB00010B/1478